Running in the Back of the Pack

A Memoir

Bettie Wailes

Other books by Bettie Wailes

SAT Words—Prioritized, a vocabulary study guide for the SAT
SAT Grammar—Prioritized, a grammar study guide for the SAT
    (to be released summer of 2014)

Contributor to:

    Chicken Soup for the Soul: Runner
    Chicken Soup for the Soul: Grandmothers
    Chicken Soup for the Soul: Grieving and Recovery

Running in the Back

of the Pack

A Memoir

Bettie Wailes

Running in the Back of the Pack

Wise Owl Publishing
925 S. Semoran Blvd, Suite 104
Winter Park, FL 32792

ISBN: 978-1-938464-02-7

Front cover photo by Mark S. Allen.

Acknowledgments

I am deeply indebted to my writing critique group—Fran, Doug, Kathleen, Teresa, and Nylda—for encouraging me and forcing me to answer the hard questions.

A special thank you to all the runners with whom I've shared the roads and trails. All of you continue to teach me, inspire me, and give me joyful memories.

Most of all, I thank RunnerDude Jim Simpson, who has made my life-long dreams a reality. He gives me joy beyond measure and makes me a better person.

CHAPTER ONE

I never thought I'd be a runner. In fact, I never thought I'd do anything athletic. I certainly never thought I'd run a marathon. That's just crazy. For a person to run more than two hundred marathons, at least one in every state—twice—would be just plain abnormal. But as it turns out, I've done exactly that. At sixty-nine, I'm still going, even if I am slowing more each year.

How then did this happen? It did not result from any grand scheme, but rather from a series of unplanned events over a number of years.

In high school, I was not one of the popular kids, and thus never in any danger of being considered for Most Likely to Succeed or Best Personality or Wittiest. However, had there been a title such as Least Athletic, I would have been a strong contender.

Home was Ferriday, a small farming town in northeast Louisiana. It never entered my mind to participate in sports, or indeed anything related to athletic activity. Neither of my parents cared for such things, nor many of my friends. I simply didn't see the point. I'm sure my lack of interest was partially because our Physical Education teacher gave so little attention to the weak, uncoordinated girls, a group for which I was the archetype. Nearly all of Coach Martha's attention was directed to her star athletes, leaving the rest of us pretty much on our own.

Therefore, in PE classes, my reputation ensured that I was nearly always the last one selected for any team.

"You have to take Bettie this time," said athletic girl number one.

"But all she'll do is sit out in left field and make clover chains," said athletic girl number two.

"I know, but it's your turn. I had to put up with her yesterday."

And so it went, time after time, regardless of the game.

1

The other girls quickly gave up trying to get me to participate, much less care about winning. *What difference does it make if I chase after a stupid ball?*

The only thing I ever did that might be labeled exercise was to march in the band, although that bit of activity was meager. First, my flute weighed less than a pound, and second, football season was only about ten weeks long.

What I *did do* was get married much too young, only to soon discover that I had married an irresponsible alcoholic who couldn't hold a steady job. It took more than seven years of his broken promises for me to conclude that he was never going to "straighten up and fly right," as he continually promised. Now with two daughters, I began to look for a way out of the despair that my life had become.

The problem was that there was no job available for which I qualified that would come close to covering the most basic living expenses. Much searching revealed that the only prudent course of action was to get an education. As daunting as that seemed, I found a way to start college, and managed to get both my degree and a divorce. After graduation from the University of Southern Mississippi in Hattiesburg, my daughters and I moved to Orlando, Florida.

I had earned a degree in mathematics and there were teaching jobs in Orlando. I found a position right away, which enabled me to establish a home for my daughters and me, and to start repaying student loans. However, after only a year and a half, I was laid off during the recession of 1975-76. Considering how hard it had been to earn the degree to teach, losing my job seemed like a cruel twist of fate. Yet I eventually came to appreciate that layoff, because it led to a job as a software engineer, a position that not only paid much better than teaching, but also suited my personality better.

Meanwhile, I had joined a great singles group in a local church. Because many of the members had children, the group planned a number of activities that included the kids. It was a great way for me to enjoy adult friends without being away from my daughters. It was where I met Judy Neuman, whose friendship was destined to become the most enduring of my life. Two of her daughters were the same ages as my daughters, so they also became close friends.

Our singles group wanted to raise money to help another member, Carol, who had been given the chance to attend seminary, but needed help with moving expenses. Mike King, bicycle mechanic, Jaycee, and member of our group, had helped the Jaycees organize a twenty-four-hour bicycle race to raise money for Muscular Dystrophy.

At a covered-dish dinner, Mike stood up. "I have an idea for how we can raise money for Carol. I think we should enter a women's team in the Jaycees bike race. The prize is five hundred dollars."

Judy asked, "Why do you think we can win?"

"There is only one other women's team entered so far."

"Well, how does it work?"

"Each eight-member team takes turns on one bike for twenty-four hours. The team with the most laps wins. The other women's team isn't very good. I think we stand a good chance of beating them. Of course, I'll provide the racing bike and I'll coach the team."

Only a handful of us women were under thirty-five, not significantly overweight, and in good health. At thirty-two and healthy, I felt obligated to participate if we agreed to this task. Judy had some athletic background, having been a competitive swimmer in her teens, and a few of the other women talked about their experiences in sports. But I had no experience whatsoever to prepare me for this bike race. My inadequacy and fear of failing made my insides knot up. But my desire not to disappoint the group was even stronger, and I agreed to ride. These people had become my family. I owed it to them to try.

The race started at nine o'clock Saturday morning and would go until nine on Sunday morning. Similar to car racing, each team was given a pit area with enough space to put up a small tent for the riders and support crew. That's where teams would change riders and attend to the bike. Each rider was to stay on the team's bike for as many of the 1.2-mile loops as possible before pulling into the pit, when the next rider would get on.

We arrived at about eight, brought our chairs and coolers into the tent, and prepared to get underway. One quick look at the other competitors and we knew we were in trouble. Most of the men's teams had genuine biking gear, such as padded bike shorts, colorful shirts with the pocket in the back, sleek helmets, bike shoes that snapped into toe clips, etc. We were in our best khaki shorts and sneakers, and our bike's pedals had no toe clips, or even toe cages. We didn't see the other two women's teams. Nonetheless, we were ready to give it our best.

With little preparation, our team of eight set out to keep the bicycle in motion for twenty-four hours. To say we didn't know what we were in for

3

would be a gross understatement. During our last planning session, we had agreed that each rider would stay on the bike for about an hour. With eight of us on the team, each rider would have a seven-hour rest. Sounded great.

The reality was that most of us stayed on for only about twenty minutes, so each rider's rest time was *much* shorter than we had planned.

As my quads burned and my arms tired, I looked at the stronger riders in amazement. *How can they keep going so fast?* It still didn't occur to me that perhaps they had actually trained for this event. *It's only because they're men.* The only good news was that the other two women's teams looked as worn out as we did.

Our short turns on the bike weren't too bad during the day, but by about two in the morning, we were not only worn out from having ridden all day, but also sleepy, and our adrenaline reserves nearly used up. In other words, we became zombies.

We somehow got through the event, and we even won the $500! But not without a price. By Sunday afternoon, it felt as though lactic acid had eaten clean through my muscles. My legs were so sore I thought it might be less painful to simply cut them off. I feared that the feeble shuffle I had adopted would be permanent. It took Epsom salt baths and days of recuperation to heal my beat-up muscles and to be able to walk normally.

However, when the same event came around the next year, our team decided to enter again, but with a different approach. We competed mostly for pride this time, the prize money an afterthought. Also, we started training three months prior to the race.

Each of us rode on our own during the week, but met each Saturday afternoon to ride together as a team, Mike again providing the coaching.

This marked the first time in my life that I actually trained for a physical competition. Expecting it to be dull, I went into it despairing that I could ever improve my performance. No one could have been more surprised than I was to discover that on some days, I actually enjoyed the practice and could see progress. During the group sessions, it was unexpectedly fun to compete with the other women.

Race day found us much more ready than the previous year. Our training showed in our improved times. Again we won, and with far less pain than the previous year.

About two months into training for the third year's race, I set out to do eight one-mile laps around the perimeter of my apartment complex. It was one of those wondrous evenings when my body functioned nearly perfect, the bike moving so fast it felt as though it hovered over the surface instead of touching the ground. Each lap was faster than the one before. On the final lap, which promised to be the fastest one of all, I rounded a turn and unintentionally headed directly into a wet patch.

One second I was sailing, euphoric at my performance, and the next I was on the ground. The bike had slid to my right and my body to the left. My left arm had splayed up so that the underside of my left elbow and my left knee took the full force of the pavement. It happened so fast that I couldn't process it for what seemed like minutes, although it was only seconds. The first thought I remember was, *I must be scraped, but I don't want to know how badly.* There was no pain yet, because my body was still in shock. I was afraid to look, hoping what I didn't know wouldn't hurt me. Slowly at first, I picked myself up and made sure my legs still worked. I probably should have been at least a little concerned about the bike, but I wasn't. My focus narrowed to one goal: getting in and out of the shower before the abraded skin began to sting. I picked up the bike and walked it back to my apartment.

I threw open the front door and, passing by the living room, yelled to my daughters that I was heading to the shower. The hope of getting out of the shower before the pain set in was dashed the moment the water hit my skin. I didn't have to look to know where I was hurt. My left knee and left elbow screamed at me. Or maybe it was me screaming.

A few minutes after I was out of the shower and trying to tend to the scrapes, my friend Judy called. When I told her I had fallen, she insisted I go to the emergency room to get checked out. I protested because I thought she was being unnecessarily cautious, but I had little choice once she showed up at my door and pulled me out to her car. Two hours and as many X-rays later, we knew she had been right. A bone in my upper arm was chipped. A cast wasn't necessary, but the arm had to remain in a sling and immobile for six weeks. I was instructed to not use the muscles in my upper arm, or else the bone chip would not remain seated properly.

The bike fared a bit better than my body. It needed only minor repairs by Mike to get it back in good condition.

Since the race was only four weeks away, my injury wouldn't be healed in time for me to ride. Still wanting to be involved, I became part of the pit crew. My daughter Karen and Judy's daughter Linda were both riding that year, and I certainly wanted to be there to support them.

The race was held in a new location, and the lap for this course was a two-mile oval. Mike was again the team coach and therefore the one with a walkie-talkie to talk with race officials. During the middle of the night, we got word that the rider on our team had fallen on the far side of the loop. Karen and Linda were napping; I was relieved it wasn't either of them. Still, I was worried about the rider who *was* out there, another teenager.

Since I was the only person awake besides Mike, I started running toward the girl. Not only was I worried about possible injuries, but a bike down meant lost time in the race. After only a short distance, my ragged breathing forced me to slow and then to walk. *What's wrong with me? Why can't I run this far? I need to get there—NOW.*

Feeling as though I were running headlong into a gale-force wind, I alternated running and walking, the running getting slower and slower, but I finally reached the rider. Fortunately, she had only minor scrapes, and was more worried about the bike than her injuries. With my one good arm, I helped her walk the bike back to the pit area so Mike could check out the bike and get the next rider going. We lost credit for the lap and we lost the time it took for me to get to the rider and for us to get back to the pit. I felt guilty that my slowness had cost us valuable time. But more than that, I kept thinking about how difficult it had been for me to run that short distance— less than a quarter of a mile. Only a year earlier, I had felt as though my body had acquired a modicum of athletic ability, and yet that night I felt as though I were right back to zero.

By now the year was 1978 and my thirty-fourth birthday was fast approaching. A part of a systems engineering team at a large defense company in Orlando, my group worked in a small, two-story outbuilding. Hardly anyone used the single, tiny elevator, but took the stairs instead. One day soon after the bike race, I realized that going up just that one flight of stairs usually left me winded.

A couple of months after the bike race, I had to visit the office of a subcontractor located on the third floor of a large office building. There was no elevator. Granted I was carrying a heavy briefcase, but by the time I reached the third floor, I was embarrassed to open the door and be seen panting and sweating. I waited in the stairwell for several minutes until my breathing slowed.

Shouldn't I be able to walk up stairs without such gasping?

I was in good health and average weight. In the span of only a few months, it had come to my attention three times that strenuous activity was far more difficult than it should have been. *What's wrong with me?*

Jim Fixx's *The Complete Book of Running* had been on the bestseller list for a year, along with the newly-released *The Aerobics Way* by Kenneth Cooper. The terms "aerobic" and "jogging" had recently entered the mainstream vocabulary. Both books had been talked about extensively on TV—and in my work group.

My desk was at the end of one of the two rows that my group of six occupied. I was the only woman. One day John leaned back in his chair, rested his legs on the corner of his desk, and tilted his head to one side as he stroked his wiry beard. "Cooper says two miles three times a week is enough to achieve and maintain cardio-vascular health."

Jim nodded and the eyebrows on his shiny, baby face rose. "Yeah, I read that, too. So do you run now?"

"No, not me." John looked my way. "How about you, Bettie?"

"No, I've never run. But lately I've been thinking I must need some kind of exercise. Just going up the stairs makes me out of breath."

Everyone nodded their heads thoughtfully. Howard said he played tennis occasionally, and Glenn said he rode his bike most weekends. Even though Jim was the only one who actually *did* run, they were unanimous in their sudden belief that *I* should run. The only requirements, they pointed out, were shoes and a street. No partners. No reservations. No memberships. No expensive equipment.

It sounded easy enough. Just get some running shoes and head out the door. I decided I'd do it. I had no way of knowing that that one seemingly casual decision would shape the rest of my life.

Jim suggested I go to Track Shack, a running specialty store that had recently opened in Orlando. He said they'd not only guide me to the right shoes, but also advise me on how to get started. A few days later, my mouth gaped open as I surveyed strange-looking shoes with unfamiliar names—Adidas, Nike, Saucony, Asics, Reebok—and prices that were equally as unfamiliar. These shoes were more expensive than entire outfits I'd bought. I picked up a few and saw that the construction was different from any shoe I'd seen. Running shoes weren't just another pair of sneakers. They were much more.

While I waited for someone to help me select shoes, I browsed the clothes. I discovered that running shorts typically have a built-in liner, or

7

brief, and a small key pocket. I saw bras made especially for running, and I learned that the tank tops runners wear are called singlets. I was indeed a stranger in a strange land. Or was it a brave new world?

As I tried several pairs of shoes, the salesclerk narrowed the choices to ones he thought would be best for me. Some didn't fit my foot very well, and others seemed too stiff. The salesclerk watched me walk and listened to my reactions.

"You need a combination of stability and flexibility," he said.

"Most of these don't feel much different than ordinary sneakers."

"Believe me, you'll notice the difference when you run in them."

An hour later, I walked out of the store with my first pair of Sauconys tucked under my arm, along with a pair of running shorts, a running bra, and a couple of singlets. What I neglected to get was advice on how to get started.

I decided to do only one mile at first, and build up to the two miles recommended by Cooper. I knew nothing about warming up, stretching, or pacing. I thought running meant full bore, all out *running*.

I put on my new shorts and singlet, laced up my Sauconys, and sped from the front door right out onto the street, intending to run the one-mile loop I had measured with my car. I don't know why I had such confidence I could finish a mile at that pace, but I shouldn't have been surprised that after passing only five houses, I was struggling to get air. Maybe I thought the running shoes would give me special powers. Clearly, I had forgotten my experience at the bike race.

I can't do this... (gasp) ... This is hard.

I walked until I could breathe again—about twenty yards. My lungs burned as I gulped air. *Why can't I do this?* Half walking, half running, my thinking changed to *I will not turn around. I will not go down in defeat. I just need to get my breath.*

A quarter mile later, however, I did give up and straggled home, breathing heavily the entire way. *Why did I think this would be easy? I guess I forgot how hard it was that night when I ran to the fallen bike rider.* Nevertheless, I felt self-conscious, as if everyone on the street knew my plans and saw that I was soundly defeated.

Two days later, I went out for another try, even though my legs were still slightly sore from the first attempt. This time I started out slower, and so I was able to go a bit farther before having to walk. My goal was now to finish *one* mile without stopping. I'd worry later about the two miles. I still had to walk to catch my breath every so often, but I completed the mile. At least I hadn't given up this time. My head didn't hang quite as low as it had two days earlier.

The milestone of running the entire mile was reached in "only" two months, and even then it was because of a dog. My younger daughter Linda was fourteen. Quite surprisingly, when she saw me getting ready to go for a run, she asked, "Mom, you don't mind if Nicki and I run with you, do you?" Nicki was Linda's dog.

"No, I don't mind." *Of course I don't mind. Why would I mind you and your dog slowing me down.* Thinking back, I can't imagine why I expected Linda to slow me down. I wasn't exactly setting any land speed records. In truth, I was probably embarrassed at the prospect of Linda seeing me wheeze and pant, and once again stop short of my goal.

Linda and Nicki annoyed me at first, because Nicki tugged Linda off course to explore smells and sounds. *There goes the dog again. I'll just go slow enough that they can catch up to me.* The first few times this happened, I resented the delays. By the fourth or fifth time, though, I changed my mind. Going slower wasn't so bad, because not once had I been forced to a walk—a first. We finished the mile and a little more without stopping.

My heart raced, this time not from exertion but from exhilaration. *Woo-hoo!* Finally, the whole mile without stopping.

We walked around the block to cool down. "Linda, to tell the truth, I wasn't thrilled about you and Nicki coming along. But now I'm grateful you did. Nicki just taught me something about running. Slow has its benefits."

What I learned that day is something most people probably learned in high school, but not me. Running full out is for sprinters, but the slower pace that Nicki forced works much better for longer distances. (Although I couldn't possibly know then how relative the word "long" is when speaking of running distances.)

Now that I could do a mile continuously, I added a little distance each week until I finally reached my original goal of two miles. Having learned about pacing, this happened relatively quickly; it took only about three weeks. Staying with the three-times-a-week plan, I usually ran on Tuesday, Thursday, and either Saturday or Sunday.

After a few months, my cardio-vascular system had improved. Going up stairs didn't leave me as breathless as before, and I felt good that I was doing something beneficial, something good for my health.

But I now had a different problem. My knees hurt. At first, I noticed the pain only when I ran, but then I started to feel it while going up the stairs, too.

Maybe I'm not meant to run.

CHAPTER TWO

One morning when I was rubbing my knee after going up the stairs, I mentioned the pain to Jim, the only runner I knew. He asked me to stand up and take a couple of steps. He watched my legs and feet. "It looks like you pronate."

"I do what?"

"Take a step very slowly. Notice how straight your ankle is when your heel first touches the ground? But as you put weight on your foot, your ankle rolls inward. That's called pronation. You probably need orthotics."

"What are orthotics?" I had a lot to learn.

"Shoe inserts that stabilize your feet. I'll give you the name of my podiatrist."

"Well, thanks for telling me I'm twisted."

"Okay, wise guy. Just go see the podiatrist."

A few days later, the doctor inspected the wear pattern on my shoes, and then had me walk on a treadmill as he carefully observed my ankles and feet. "Uh-huh. Just as I thought."

"What?"

"You pronate."

"Yeah, that's what my friend said. Is this a common problem?"

"More than half the population pronate, at least to some degree. Smaller groups either supinate or have ankles that remain vertical."

"What does it mean to suppinate?"

"Suppination is the opposite of pronation—the foot rolls outward. The reason either one causes knee pain is that when the ankle falls to one side, it causes the shin bone to rotate in the knee socket. The continual rotation of the tibia, step after step, irritates the knee socket and causes pain.

"For a pronator, the orthotic is thicker on the inside, preventing the foot from rolling inward as much. That should alleviate your knee pain."

He made plaster casts of my feet that would be used to mold the orthotics. Before I left, he recommended no running until after the orthotics came in, to allow my knees a chance to heal a bit.

At the next appointment three weeks later, I saw that the three layers of molded plastic included a middle layer of a spongy material, much thicker along the inside of the heel and midfoot.

With the orthotics in my shoes, I walked around the podiatrist's office while he watched. He pointed out that my ankles only barely fell to the inside. He recommended an adjustment period to allow my muscles and joints to become accustomed to the inserts. He said a few people wear them all the time, but most wear them only when running.

Soon after getting home, I went out for a short, three-quarter mile run. During the time off from running, the knee pain had subsided. Now I expected it to return, but it didn't.

The next morning, I waited to feel the usual pain while walking up the stairs, but it never came. In three weeks, I was back to my full two-mile loop, and felt no soreness in my knees. The effect of the orthotics was extraordinary. No longer concerned about my knees, I was free to run regularly.

~ ~ ~

It was Christmas, 1978. I picked up my last present—the most mysterious one. The heavy package was an odd size. I peeled back the red paper and saw a box remarkably like the one my daughter Karen's last pair of boots had come in. *I know she didn't get me boots.* I broke the tape on the box, lifted the lid, dug through layers of tissue paper and found Jim Fixx's *The Complete Book of Running.*

"Oh, Karen, this *is* a nice surprise." It was special because she had selected it on her own; it wasn't on my "hint" list. It was even more special because it indicated her support of my running.

"I hope you like it," Karen said, with a hopeful smile.

"According to the guys at work, this is the best book for a beginning runner." Still new at running, I had a lot to learn and thought this was the book to teach me.

Karen seemed pleased that I liked her choice.

I dove into Jim Fixx's book right away, hoping to find . . . well, I wasn't sure what I'd find. Fixx pointed out many advantages of running: ability to achieve and maintain healthy weight, increased sense of well-being, improved cardio-vascular health, and—here's the one that got my attention—the ability to function better with less sleep. I did maintain my weight, but then I'd never battled a serious weight problem. I enjoyed an increased sense of well-being that came with the feeling of accomplishment each time I met a goal. I felt healthier than before I started running. I could walk up stairs without getting as winded.

But the promise about less sleep never came about for me. Fixx contended that a more healthy person required less sleep than a less healthy one. I had always required a lot of sleep, so I thought if I could get by on less, even one hour less, I'd have extra time in my day. But that never happened. In fact, the harder I trained, the more sleep I needed to recover, and still do.

For the next few years, my running cycled on and off. Because I'm not a morning person, I ran in the evening. But if overtime was required, it would be too late to run when I got home. Taking a night class precluded running on those evenings. Dinner with friends meant a skipped run. After a week or more of skipped runs, the habit was gone.

After each lapse, though, something indescribable drew me back. Maybe it was missing the alleged endorphins, although I can't say I've ever been aware of a so-called "endorphin rush." Maybe it was because I missed the smell of sweat. Maybe it was simply guilt for not doing what I had come to think of as an obligation, a duty to self. Perhaps something subtle had happened in the way I thought of myself, which included the label "runner." Whatever it was, some force pulled me back.

In early 1983, after five years of intermittent running, my job took me to the Dallas-Ft. Worth area for an extended period. Now working for a different company, I was one of a handful of engineers sent to install and test a flight simulator. We worked long hours, and at the end of most days, the group went directly from work to dinner. When I finally reached my hotel at nine or ten, I was too full and too tired to run. Besides, it wouldn't have been safe at that late hour.

One day when I hadn't run in several weeks, I thought I heard a sigh coming from my forsaken running shoes. I looked at the shoes and then asked myself, "How important is running to me?" *If it's really important, I need to commit to a time of day when other things won't interfere.* Some part of me believed that running was important enough to find a time.

Since evenings weren't working out, only one other time of day was left—early morning. As I've said, I'm not a morning person. I've been accused of being semi-comatose for the first hour of the day. But I thought if I could just get up and out the door without stopping to think about it, I'd be finished and back in before I was fully awake.

That worked for a while. The early alarm got me up and out the door on my running days for a few weeks. Then one morning after working unusually late, I slapped off the alarm, craving sleep more than running. This sound logic made it easier to switch off the alarm the next time. I stopped setting it for the early time.

After a couple of weeks off, though, the road tugged at me, and once again I managed to pull myself out of bed to the screeching clock. This pattern continued—weeks of disciplined running followed by a week or two off. However, each time I fell into idleness, that inexplicable force pulled me back to the roads. This cycle continued for another year.

On Sunday, August 5, 1984, I was in one of those "idle" periods. I had slept late. After making coffee, I turned on the TV, hoping to see more gymnastics in the Los Angeles Summer Olympics. But the event being broadcast wasn't gymnastics—it was the first-ever Olympic women's marathon. It was about fifteen minutes before the start.

CHAPTER THREE

Even before the race started, the coverage reached out and pulled me in. I moved from the TV only to get coffee. Before and during the race, I gave my rapt attention to every word from the commentators.

When the announcers talked about the distance of 26.2 miles, I thought that couldn't be right. People can't actually run twenty-six miles. Not all on the same day.

I was wrong.

I had heard of a long race called the marathon, but I never paid attention to the actual distance or to the story behind the event. As I listened to the description of the event, I was captivated. In 490 B.C. the Greek messenger Pheidippides ran from the battlefield at Marathon to Athens—about twenty-five miles—to deliver the news that the Greeks had defeated the Persians at Marathon. He had just run a distance of a hundred forty miles during the previous two days, so when he reached Athens, he collapsed—and died from exhaustion, or so one version of the story goes. The first modern marathon was run in 1886, with a distance of twenty-six miles. When the race was run in London in 1908, the distance was extended by 385 yards so the race could finish in front of the royal family's viewing box, making the distance exactly 26.2 miles. This has remained the marathon distance since.

I'd never heard of any of the marathon participants, but now that I was a runner—well, sort of—I listened to the back-stories about the competitors, and about the history of women's running. One of the commentators was Kathrine Switzer. The other commentator, Jim Lampley, reminded viewers that Kathrine had been the first woman to officially run the Boston Marathon in 1977. [1]

---

[1] Women had been completely barred from marathons until the sixties. Among the reasons cited was that their uteruses could fall out. In 1967 Kathrine Switzer became the first woman to officially run the Boston Marathon. Because she had

That was only seven years ago. And now there's a women's marathon in the Olympics. Things have changed quickly. Lampley explained how that first Boston finish had led to much greater acceptance of women in the running community in general.

Not until years later, after learning more about the history of women's running and Switzer's role in getting the women's marathon into the Olympics, did I fully appreciate the significance of hearing her commentary that day.

The barring of women from marathons was only one of the many barriers that fell in the seventies. I remembered the advice I had received in 1970 when I told two engineers I was considering changing my major from mathematics to engineering. They both advised against it, though, saying that because I was female, I'd never get a job as an engineer. The most I could hope for was to be an assistant engineer. But in 1977, I *had* gotten a job as a software engineer, on the strength of my math degree. Things were changing rapidly in many areas, including, apparently, the running world. I had some grasp of the excitement that the women runners must have felt in that first event for women.

I heard the gun signifying that the race was underway, and the announcers followed each runner in the small field with great interest.

Joan Benoit just passed up the first water stop. She might regret that later. It's a hot day, and so it's important to stay hydrated.

Yes, and as we've seen before, the runner who goes to the front in the beginning often fades in the later miles. It's important to control the pace in a race this long.

Well, she is the clear leader for now with a six-second lead.

I thought back to my first attempts to run only *one* mile, and how I had learned the foolishness of starting out too fast. I tried to compare my own experience to that of a marathoner, but it was no use. I simply couldn't imagine running so far.

---

been using only her initials as her byline (she was a journalism major), she registered as K. V. Switzer. The race officials were unaware a woman had registered. Once an official recognized she was female, he grabbed her and tried to pull her from the course. Her two-hundred-forty-pound boyfriend blocked the official and Switzer finished the marathon in four hours twenty minutes.

In 1972, six women competed in the New York City Marathon, but staged a protest of the ruling that they must start the race ten minutes ahead of the men. They sat until the time elapsed, then got up and started with the men.

For those of you who don't know, Joan missed some training earlier this year because of knee surgery. In fact, she won the Olympic trials only seventeen days after that procedure.

Yes, that was certainly a remarkable recovery. Let's hope the knee holds up today.

Something else I couldn't imagine. How could she recover quickly enough to race in just seventeen days? A late night out dancing was enough to prevent me from putting on running shoes.

Right behind Joan, the lead pack included Grete Waitz, Rosa Mota, Ingrid Kristiansen, Priscilla Welch, and Lorraine Moller, all well-known names in the running world, but ones I had not heard before.

Joan is approaching mile sixteen, and has increased her lead. If someone is going to make a move, I'd think it would be soon.

That's right. If the rest of the lead pack lets her get too far ahead, they won't be able to catch her in the later miles, when the heat and fatigue will set in.

We could see Greta Waitz or Ingrid Kristiansen break away any time now.

But none of the other women went after Joan, and she didn't wilt as the commentators had feared. Instead, in her now-famous white painter's cap, she conquered mile after mile, despite the conditions. She was steady and relentless. The temperature reached into the eighties that day, which is hot for road racing at any distance, but even more extreme for a distance of that length. The runners would have preferred at least twenty degrees cooler. The temperature was an even more formidable foe because the course offered no protection from the August California sun.

Despite her recent surgery and the brutal race conditions, Joan maintained her pace, mile by mile, increasing her lead. During the last miles, some runners dropped out. Others slowed far behind their usual pace. But Joan didn't falter as she continued inexorably toward the finish line in the Los Angeles Coliseum. The last mile of the course took the runners from the street through a tunnel into the coliseum, and then one full lap around the track to the finish line.

The crowds rose to their feet when Joan entered the coliseum. Her face was deadpan and her focus straight ahead until the final straightaway, when she broke into a smile and waved her white cap to the crowd. The world witnessed not only a great moment in the history of women's running—the first-ever Olympic women's marathon—but also a performance that would have been judged extraordinary because of the extreme circumstances. She finished with a time of 2:24, at the time the third fastest women's marathon time on record.

As Joan crossed the finish line, my breath caught in my throat, and I felt something close to tremors flowing through my body, almost as if it had been my victory, too. I cried in exultation for Joan—a woman I'd never heard of before that morning in an event I had known nothing about a mere three hours earlier.

I remained transfixed as other runners entered the coliseum. Tears of sympathy fell for the women who had a difficult time, or didn't finish at all.

The camera focused on one runner in particular—Switzerland's Gabriele Andersen-Scheiss—who clearly suffered from heat exhaustion. Nearing the coliseum, she staggered as if she were intoxicated, one arm stiff, the other swaying limply, and one leg dragging. As she entered, paramedics rushed to her and tried to pull her from the course to give her aid. She motioned them away, knowing if she were aided, she'd be disqualified. She insisted on completing that final lap. The hushed crowd watched breathlessly during the minutes it took for her to make her way around the track to the finish line. She staggered the last few yards, where she collapsed into the arms of the paramedics. As they tended to her, the crowd gave her a standing ovation for her valiant effort. The heat's effect was also evident on the faces of many others as they struggled to the finish.

And yet there had been Joan, still able to take the American flag on a victory lap around the track. Normally resistant to celebrity, I now had an idol.

Twenty minutes after the coverage ended, I remained riveted to my seat, allowing the impact to settle over me. *How can anyone run twenty-six miles?*

Suddenly their spirit ignited something inside me. I bound out of my chair. *If they can run that far, surely I can run farther than three miles.*

Over the previous few years, my normal distance had gradually been extended from the original two miles. As others had predicted, I couldn't resist the challenge of going a bit farther occasionally, but not by much.

Drawing strength and resolve from those women, I dried my tears, put on my shorts, laced up my shoes, and headed out to the pathway that wound through my apartment complex and into the adjoining neighborhood. At the edge of the running trail, I readied myself. With her image fresh in my mind, I tried to simulate Joan Benoit's form as I started my run.

Her shoulders didn't rotate, and she held her hands about waist high. She kept her body upright, with her shoulders relaxed and eyes looking straight ahead. She didn't lean forward like a sprinter.

In my mind's eye, I looked like Joan, except for the white painter's cap. I was sure I had the same relaxed form, the same easy stride. Never mind that my miles took twice as long as hers—nine minutes or longer. If only I had that cap! Or could it be the shoes?

In truth, I grew tired after the usual distance, but I couldn't shake the images of the marathoners. Instead of taking the shortest route back to my apartment, I kept thinking of Joan, and pushed through one more loop to complete a staggering four miles.

I could train hard and enter a road race some day. I could get better shoes, better shorts, and maybe a painter's cap.

The fantasy ran wild for a few minutes. Then I was home. Inside, I looked in the mirror.

Forty years old and slow. Who am I kidding?

CHAPTER FOUR

Four years and two jobs later, in 1988, a coworker discovered that I ran, and seemed to think I should enter a road race. I had long since forgotten the daydream of running like Joan Benoit, or training for a race. I was too old to compete—especially for the first time.

"But, Shane," I said as I looked up at him from my desk chair, "I'm not a real runner. I just make my way around the neighborhood."

The truth was that I thought of myself as a casual jogger, and feared competing with "real" runners. I hadn't recognized my competitive nature before, but my ego couldn't withstand the sure humiliation of being slower than everyone else.

Shane stood with a hand on his hip, looking down at me with the kind of expression one uses when explaining something to a child. "Believe me, Bettie, all kinds of people run in these road races. Come on, give it a try."

"But what if I'm the last one to finish? I'd be humiliated."

Shane sat down and leaned forward. "Judging from what you've said about your training times, I know you wouldn't be last."

"Training times? You have me confused with a real athlete. I merely get my feet on the ground a few times a week just to get my heart rate up. I'll leave the competition for you young, thirty-something guys."

He shook his head as he gave up and walked away.

Shane had already told me about his times in local road races; he often placed in the top three in his highly-competitive thirty to thirty-four age group. Occasionally he placed in the top three *overall*. If his time for a 5K[2] was over sixteen minutes, he was disappointed. He ran a mile in barely over five minutes. That sounded incredibly impressive, considering Roger Bannister's four-minute mile had set a world record. I, on the other hand, usually ran a mile in about nine minutes. My times clearly said I was not a real runner.

---

[2] Common road race distances are 5Kilometers (3.1 miles) and 10K (6.2 miles).

21

But Shane was persistent. A month later, he walked into my office and slapped a race application on my desk. "Okay, here's a little 5K in a small town west of here. It's a Fourth of July run, only a month away. If you enter, I promise I'll run with you. That way, you can't be last." The expression on his face made his statement sound dangerously close to a dare.

Why is he so determined for me to enter a road race? He must really believe I'd enjoy it if he's willing to slow down to my pace and stay with me.

"But, Shane, I'm not as fast as those people. And you'd have to slow down a lot to stay with me."

"Look, Bettie, not all the runners are the same pace. People of many ages and speeds will be there. Besides, you wouldn't have to *win* or anything to enjoy the race."

His willingness to sacrifice a race told me how eager he was for me to enter. Curiosity about what I was missing won out.

I sent in the form.

On July 4, 1988, I drove my forty-three-year-old body to the race site and looked for the parking directions Shane had assured me I'd see.

I forgot to ask if there would be toilets available. If not, I'm in trouble, from both the coffee and the nerves.

Pondering my potential predicament, I saw the promised parking signs. While I looked for an empty space, my muscles twitched and my stomach churned. Pulling into a spot, I looked around at the other runners. Some pinned on numbers, some adjusted shoes, some did short sprints or stretched. They had one thing in common—they all looked as if they knew what they were doing.

In contrast, I had no idea what I should be doing. I felt as though I had a neon sign on my forehead flashing "NEW RUNNER." I had never stretched prior to a run, but wondered if that was what I should do, until I remembered I didn't know what stretches to do. Then I saw Shane's car.

Thank Goodness, Shane's here. He'll know what to do.

Shane parked close by and walked over, looking quite different in running clothes. He didn't seem to notice that I looked different, too. "Hey, Shane, are there bathrooms here?"

"Sure, there's a row of port-a-potties over there. See the bank of green?"

"Oh, I see them now. That's going to be my first stop."

"Then we'll find the packet pick-up area and get our race packets. After that, we'll come back to our cars to pin on our race numbers and stash the packets."

"What are race packets?"

"Usually a large brown envelope that contains your race number, pins to attach your number to your shirt, and other stuff."

"Another question." I lowered my voice. "Should I stretch? I've never stretched before."

"No, don't do anything new. Ignore what everybody else is doing—just do what you do before your runs at home."

Back at my car with race packet in hand, I was surprised to find many items in the race packet—a sample of runner's lubricant, a mini energy bar, flyers about upcoming events, etc. Shane explained that this packet actually contained fewer such items than the packets for larger races.

At home, I normally walked around the house a little before running, enough to get the blood flowing. Once outside, I started out slowly. After our numbers were on, I told Shane my routine. He approved, so we jogged slowly to warm up. Shane stayed with me as I pretended I knew what I was doing.

About ten minutes prior to start time, the voice of the race announcer came over the speakers. "Runners, it's time to move to the start line. Please line up according to pace."

I asked Shane what the announcer meant. He explained that runners are requested to line up with the fastest runners up front and the slowest in the back. Shane guided us to about two-thirds back into the line-up.

"Are we far enough back? I think I'm pretty slow."

"I guarantee the only people behind us are either *very* slow runners or walkers. We'll be fine."

The gun went off, and Shane cautioned me not to go out too fast. "Just run like you do at home. Let the rabbits go ahead. You'll probably pass some of them before the end."

I could see it required effort for him to go at my slow pace, but he didn't complain. As we approached the end of the first mile, I was surprised to see someone calling out times. Shane explained that at many races, the split time[3] is called at each mile. Mine was faster than I expected—8:35.

---

[3] A split time is the time into the race at a segment of the full distance, usually at each mile. For example, the time I heard at mile two is the time it took me to reach that point on the course.

After the two-mile split, Shane said, "Hey, you're maintaining a nice even pace. That's good. Just keep this going for one more mile." I don't remember if I passed anyone during the last mile or not, but I made it to the end without slowing down much.

Nearing the finish line, Shane reminded me to notice my time as I crossed under the banner. At the last second, I remembered to look up at the clock. The race officials urged us to keep moving to the end of the chute, where a scoring card was handed to me. This was long before the days of electronic timing. Timing was largely on the honor system, although the race officials did keep the cards in order of finish. We were expected to watch the timing clock as we crossed the finish line, and then write our time on a card. I leaned over a nearby table and wrote my name and my time of 26:44, and headed off to find water.

To my astonishment, people were behind me. In fact, people continued to come in, even as we walked off in search of food.

Later, as we stood drinking Gatorade and eating bananas, Shane said, "We should stay for the awards ceremony. You might have placed in your age group."

"You're kidding," I smirked.

"No, I'm serious. I don't see many women who look like they're around your age."

The race application had included something about awards for the overall first, second, and third place male and female, and also to the first three finishers in each age group. My group was 40-49-year-old females. Looking around, I thought Shane could be right about there being few women in my age group. The names being called faded into the background as I became absorbed in looking at the variety of people around us. I finally understood what Shane had tried to tell me. I saw short and tall, old and young, skinny and, well, not so skinny.

While I was busy analyzing the crowd, Shane poked me and said, "Go on up."

I became vaguely aware that someone had said my name.

Shane nudged me again. "You placed second in your age group." He smiled and pointed to the announcer.

Stunned, I couldn't move at first. Believing I didn't deserve it, I reluctantly walked up to accept the award. I expected to hear someone yell, "She's an imposter, not a real runner." Instead, the crowd clapped for me just as they had done for all the other winners. My cheeks burned as I glanced at the crowd of smiling faces. Quickly looking back down, I cradled the trophy—a generic runner on top and an engraved plate announcing "2nd place, 40-49 age group"—and wondered, *Does this mean I'm an athlete?*

In the car driving home, I still didn't feel like an athlete, but I kept smiling nonetheless. And I had to admit that Shane had been right about one thing—I did enjoy the race. The sense of achievement, and the realization that I was a little better than I thought, was powerful. Tangible evidence of success lay right there on the car seat. For someone who had never entered an athletic competition, this was a major achievement.

I placed the trophy on a shelf in my family room, with no inkling how that small object would impact my life. First, I couldn't possibly know that even though this first award would always have a special place, it would be joined by many others over the coming years. Second, I didn't know how much I would come to be defined by my running.

On my usual circuit around my neighborhood the next week, I felt the urge to push a little harder than before, my competitive nature starting to emerge. While I knew I was no Joan Benoit, I *did* feel a bit more like a runner, and a bit less like a jogger.

In early August, a postcard from our local running store announced a Grand Prix Series of Running: eight races on dates from September through March. Because of the heat in the South, the race season begins in the fall and goes through the spring, avoiding the hot summer months. The number of events surprised me; I didn't expect that many races in the local area. My interest was growing fast until I saw the two 10K (6.2 mile) events. Completing three miles was challenge enough. Was six miles too much?

However, the age-group award from the July race taunted me to enter another race. Every time I looked at it, I knew I would. Even though I didn't expect to place in my age group again—after all, the July Fourth race was a very small event—I decided that merely *completing* each of the eight races in the series would be challenge enough--especially the two 10Ks. But I had to try.

The first race on the schedule was in mid-September, six weeks away. I began to log my times, and tried to shave off a few seconds with each run. I asked Shane for advice and, for the first time, actually listened when he described how he did speed work. I didn't merely go out for a run anymore. I was now training.

Meanwhile, encouragement came from an unexpected source that summer. I was a software engineer and had started a new job in May with a small defense company. The company's home office was in California; our local branch had but a single contract. The two top positions at our office were held by Kim Wilson, program manager, and Paul Quinlan, operations manager. In Central Florida, the simulation and training industry formed a fairly small community and many of us worked together at more than one company. For example, I had previously worked with Kim at two other companies.

I hadn't met Paul prior to this.

From the outset, Paul stopped by my desk more often than needed. Sometimes he checked to make sure that I had gotten a recent memo. Other times it was to tell me about a meeting—one that I already knew about. Or he had just heard a joke that he simply must share.

It didn't take long for me to get the impression that Paul's interest was more personal than business. I didn't much care for him at first, and if I had been looking for a relationship, wouldn't have been attracted to him even. But I wasn't. I had been through a series of bad relationships, and had sworn off dating—at least for a while. It wasn't his looks. Average height and weight, Paul had light brown hair, blue eyes, and an attractive smile, which his mustache accented. It was his personality that didn't appeal to me. At the time I thought of him as humorous, but with a hint of something that reminded me of someone trying too hard to sell me something. Not quite smarmy, but almost.

Months later, Paul told me he hadn't been looking for a relationship either, but was drawn to me even *before* we met.

"Before we met?" How could that be?

"I was in Kim's office the day he called you about the job. I couldn't hear your voice, but a strange feeling came over me while he was talking to you. I don't know how to describe it, except to say that I somehow knew you would be an important person in my life. I didn't know exactly how, though."

I didn't know how to respond. I tried to recall if I had ever had any similar experience.

Paul continued, "The day I met you, and I looked into your eyes, I knew we would be together. Maybe not soon, but eventually."

I was skeptical when he told me this, thinking it was just another one of his attempts to pique my interest. Over time, though, his sincerity persuaded me his experience had been real.

When his little visits began, I never for a moment considered Paul as a potential romantic interest. Even if his personality had appealed to me, he smoked. I was intolerant of smoking, partly because I was still forced to endure long meetings in closed rooms with smokers. (Smoking had not yet been banned in the workplace.) Second, he had two adolescent daughters. After a previous relationship with a man who had children, I didn't care to get involved with someone else's offspring again.

On the other hand, I couldn't bring myself to reject Paul flatly because I enjoyed his sense of humor too much. He never failed to make me laugh with a humorous story or joke. His was a sophisticated, intelligent, often dry sort of humor—and I liked it. I allowed myself to enjoy the banter with him, promising myself it would never go beyond a casual friendship. But that was a promise I was not destined to keep.

CHAPTER FIVE

One Friday evening at June's end, most of the people at our small company gathered at a neighborhood restaurant and pub. We enjoyed socializing together, and an employee's farewell gave us good reason to party. In a room reserved for our group, we started with about thirty-five people. I felt Paul's eyes on me from the beginning, but he didn't approach me directly. At least not right away. While the evening progressed, he worked his way down the long table so that he eventually sat directly across from me. Soon we found ourselves sitting apart from the other two small groups that remained. I had not exceeded my two-drink limit, and I'd had a full dinner, so I was nearly sober. Paul's drink tally was at least a half dozen, and I had not seen him eat more than a few small snacks. His eyes and his speech told me he was far too impaired to drive safely.

"Paul, how about I drive you home?"

"Thanks, but I'm all right." He turned his nearly-empty glass slowly.

"You don't look all right to me. If you have an accident on your way home, I'll never forgive myself."

"Don't worry about me. I'm experienced at this."

"You make it sound like you do this often."

"Often enough. I can manage."

I didn't care how many times he might have managed before, I only knew I couldn't have it on my conscience if he had an accident that night. I did the only other thing I could think of. I ordered coffee for both of us, and kept motioning for the server to freshen his until closing time was announced around midnight.

We carried our conversation and our to-go coffee out to my car, where we talked for two more hours. The more sober Paul got, the more serious the conversation grew, and he revealed a side of him that I hadn't so much as glimpsed before. At work and around other people, he avoided talking about himself, tending to either talk shop or be the comedian. That night, he told me about his childhood, his time in the Air Force, his marriage, his political views, and his spiritual beliefs.

As we discussed these topics, he became more engaging, especially when we got to the subjects of politics and religion. These topics, while often contentious, provided us a lot of common ground. We agreed on nearly every political issue. And we had a lot in common regarding religion, too. It turned out we had each been raised in a strict religious environment—him Catholic, me Methodist—but as adults had questioned many of the doctrines we had been taught. Surprisingly, we had each adopted some of the same non-traditional viewpoints, which we were reluctant to discuss with most people.

And I learned he was a younger man—a whole three years younger. I was then forty-four; he was only forty-one.

Not everything that I learned made him more appealing, however. He smoked. I hated smoking. He was a meat and potatoes man; he argued that ketchup was a vegetable. I was a borderline vegetarian, to which I added vitamins and other nutritional supplements. He made no effort to exercise. I ran regularly and had recently run my first 5K road race. I now planned to run all eight races in the Grand Prix Series of Running—six 5Ks and two 10Ks.

While he showed no interest in changing his habits, he commended me for my efforts—especially the running, which I found surprising.

Before we said goodnight, Paul asked if he could see me again.

"I'm not sure, Paul."

"How about just lunch? You don't have anything against having lunch with a friend, do you?"

"No, as long as you understand that we're just friends."

Even though my view of him had softened, I still had no interest in a romantic relationship. I wanted to be certain he understood that.

Meanwhile, the date of the first race in the Grand Prix Series arrived. It was the first weekend in September. This time I approached the race site with a much different attitude than I had at my first race only two months earlier. No longer a novice, I wasn't concerned about merely finishing. I was concerned about improving my time. I went through a serious pre-race routine, an amalgam gathered from runners I had observed at the first race and from Shane's advice: first jogging slowly to warm up, then doing a few stretches, and finally doing a few strides, or short bursts at top speed.

Despite the training, my time was nearly a minute slower than the first race—27:39. I had allowed my eagerness to overrule my better judgment. I went out too fast, which caused me to slow considerably in the last half. Exactly what Shane had warned me about. In the first race, I placed second out of three in my age group. In this race, seventeen women in my age group competed, and my time was again near the middle, only this time that meant seventh place. I was disappointed with my time, and surprised to see how fast some of the other women were, but decided to use those times as inspiration.

At work the following Monday, Paul surprised me by asking how the race went. I didn't expect him to remember I had planned to do a race. Not only did he remember the race, but also he remembered my time at the first race. He politely overlooked the slower time and lower standing in my age group. The sparkle in his eyes when he congratulated me on "another good performance" brought a tiny bit of warmth into my heart, in spite of my resoluteness regarding the nature of our relationship.

In the second race of the series, my eagerness and overconfidence again got the better of me. I started out too fast, faded during the last mile, and ended up with a time even slower than the first two races. In the refreshment area, two women I had seen at the last race, and who were in my age group, came over. The shorter one with light brown hair spoke first. "We noticed you over here by yourself. I'm Barbara Miller and this is Rose Reeves. Haven't we seen you at other runs?"

"I think so," I said, still breathing heavily. "I'm Bettie. I remember you both placed in our age group at the last race. I don't know how you do it. During the last mile, I just couldn't keep up the pace. My legs were tired, and I struggled to breathe."

Rose, taller than Barbara, nodded as she pushed her curly, auburn hair away from her face. "Nearly every runner knows what that's like."

Barbara replaced the cap on her water bottle. "I know I shouldn't go out too fast, but it's so hard to remember that when all the fast runners are rushing past. If my first mile is too fast, I end up losing all that time and more by the end."

I've heard that before. "I need to work on that. There's so much I don't know about running and racing."

Rose peeled a banana. "We're all still learning. It seems to be a slow process. Will we see you at the next race?"

"Yes, I hope so. The one after that is a 10K, isn't it? I've never run that far." I took a swig of water and bit into a bagel.

"Don't let that worry you. If you can run 5K, you can run 10K. Just slow your pace as you increase your distance," said Rose.

Barbara added, "But don't try to increase your distance too quickly. Go just a little farther each week."

"Thanks for the advice." I looked around at knots of other runners chatting. "I've noticed other runners encouraging each other, even on the course. Why are people so willing to help each other when they're competing on race day?"

"Most runners aren't competing with each other as much as they're competing with themselves—their own recent times," said Barbara.

Over the years I've found that most runners wish each other good luck at the start, shout encouragement on the course, and congratulate each other at the finish line. The community of runners, for the most part, do exactly as Barbara said. They don't so much complete with other runners as with the clock. Barbara and Rose were among the first to demonstrate that spirit to me, but certainly not the last.

As summer gave way to fall, Paul continued his relentless pursuit, which, because of my reluctance to go beyond friendship, required boundless patience. However, he had two effective weapons to keep my interest—his clever wit and his encouragement of my running. Each time he made me laugh, or said, "Way to go, Bettie," another tiny fissure appeared in my emotional shield.

By mid-September, he finally persuaded me to have dinner with him. Until then I had limited our meals to lunch. Lunch was just two friends; dinner was a date. But I caved in one day when he invited me to my favorite seafood restaurant. Before our meal was served, Paul took a small, gift-wrapped box from his jacket pocket. "Here's a little something to show you I'm serious."

Inside was a bracelet of three intertwined chains, in white, yellow, and pink gold. "Paul, this is beautiful, but I can't accept it. That would be giving you false encouragement."

Paul reached for my hand and sighed with impatience. His blue eyes locked onto mine as he said, "Look, Bettie, this is the way it is. I love you. . . I'll always love you." He leaned back and raised both hands palms out, as if conceding a point. "I have the rest of my life, so take your time. Meanwhile, I want you to have the bracelet. Please keep it."

I didn't know what to say. No one had ever said anything like that to me. I decided to accept the bracelet, but made no commitment. I blinked back tears and looked out the window for a moment, trying to process what had just happened.

As if that kind of pronouncement had been nothing out of the ordinary, Paul picked up the conversation as usual, demonstrating a combination of patience and faith.

I went home, with the bracelet, thinking about what he had said. *Is this man real? He seems too good to be true. There must be a catch.*

CHAPTER SIX

It took a different kind of attention from Paul for me to fully understand how genuine his affection was. I awoke one day in early October with a high fever and called in sick. Within an hour, Paul was at my house to check on me.

"You don't look good. You need to see a doctor."

"I don't feel good, either." Chills made my teeth chatter so much it was difficult to speak. "But I don't really have a doctor. The only one I've seen in the last few years is my gynecologist."

"Don't worry. I'll find someone."

He opened the phone book and began calling doctors. He found one nearby who could see me in the next hour. Following my directions, he brought clothes to me, and then respectfully turned his head while I dressed.

After driving me to the doctor's office, Paul sat in the waiting room while I saw the doctor. It turned out I had a raging kidney infection, for which the doctor prescribed antibiotics, fluids, and rest.

Paul took me home, put me to bed, and supplied me with water and Gatorade before he left to get my prescription filled. A little while later, he awakened me from my feverish stupor to give me the first dose of medicine.

He returned in the early evening with soup, crackers, and more Gatorade. He heated the soup and stayed with me while I ate it—and gave me the next dose of medicine. It was a good thing he did, because I was still so foggy from the fever that I'm not sure I would have had enough to drink, and might not have taken the medicine as prescribed.

He returned the next morning and afternoon to check on me, and to feed me more soup.

On the third day, now feeling much better, I stopped long enough to look at myself in the mirror. *How has Paul been able to look at me?* My hair was a mess, my face was even whiter than the usual pale color, and I looked

35

ten years too old. At least I could hold my head up, though, and I thought I might even be able to get in the shower.

Before I tried it, however, Paul was there to check on me.

"Feeling better?" he called from the kitchen.

I sat up. "Much." I quickly pulled the sheet over my head.

"What's wrong?" Paul asked, as he entered the bedroom.

For the first time in three days, I could make complete sentences. "I'm afraid for you to see me. You'll probably scream and go running out the door."

He laughed and pulled the sheet down. "Why worry now? You look better than you did yesterday."

"How could you stand it?"

Ignoring the question, he started gathering dirty glasses from the nightstand.

"Paul?"

"What?"

"Thank you for all this." I gestured at the room.

"All what?" He paused and registered a look of confusion.

"For taking care of me. Bringing me food. Not running away at the sight of me." I smiled.

"What else would I do?" He frowned slightly, and then shook his head. After taking a bowl and a few glasses to the kitchen, he returned and sat in a chair near the bed.

"Well, I haven't known many men would have taken so much time from work to come check on me. Nor would they have done this much for me."

He got a puzzled look on his face. "But I love you. If someone says he cares about you and yet doesn't take care of you when you're sick, either he's a fool or else he doesn't know what love is."

"Well, I guess I've known some of both kinds."

He took my hand in his. "Look, Bettie, I love you. Don't you understand? Those aren't just words."

"I can see that."

He moved to sit on the side of the bed and pulled me close. He nuzzled his chin in my hair, which was courageous considering how dirty it was. Since that first dinner in September, small pieces of my emotional shield had been quietly falling away. Now, the final piece came down, and before I knew what was happening, the words I had resisted saying slipped out. "I love you, too, Paul."

And so it was that I surrendered my heart to Paul, exposed and unprotected.

Paul celebrated every aspect of my life—my career, my daughters and grandchildren, but especially my running. He offered to go with me to races, in spite of the early start times. Most races start at seven or seven-thirty, which meant I needed to be at the race location at least an hour earlier. Since neither of us were morning people, the early hour seemed unnatural.

"I don't mind getting up as long as you're the one doing the running. I'll be the one with the camera." Paul enjoyed photography and welcomed opportunities to practice his hobby.

By the time he made this generous offer, the third race in the Grand Prix series was only a few weeks away. This was to be my first 10K—six point two miles. Could I keep going that far? It was time to find out, as my focus transitioned from speed to distance.

Until the most recent race, I had been running a three-mile route in my neighborhood. Shane had recently moved on to another company, so he was no longer there with his ready advice. But I remembered what Barbara had said about increasing the distance gradually. I added a half-mile each week, until I was up to five miles. Each time I added to the distance, I slowed my pace slightly. So far, the plan had worked; at least I had gotten through each run. With each new distance, Paul high-fived me. "That's my running girl."

Even though I'd already run five miles, doing the three-mile loop twice still seemed a little scary. I set out with a certain amount of trepidation, and mindful of keeping a comfortable pace. I couldn't pinpoint exactly what I thought might happen. *Will my legs stop working? Will I be unable to continue?* Whatever I had feared, however irrational it was, never materialized. When I passed the point I estimated to be five miles, I felt a slight quiver and took a deep breath, but kept going. I simply finished the loop the second time around, none the worse for wear.

The next day at work, Paul said, "I knew you could do it. I don't why you were so unsure of yourself."

Now confident of the distance, I worked on picking up my pace during the two weeks remaining before the 10K.

With my distance now longer, I discovered that running had an unexpected effect on my body. It stimulated my lower digestive tract. When I ran only three or four miles, I could make it home before the situation became problematic. But with longer distances, I couldn't make it the whole way without a bathroom break. I developed the habit of running a one-mile warm-up that ended back at the house, going in for a quick bathroom visit, then going back out for the rest of the run.

I mentioned this to Barbara at a road race and she said that she had done something similar for years. Discussion with a few other runners revealed that this was not unusual. *Runner's World* even ran an article about "runner's trots." I felt better knowing I wasn't alone, and I learned to plan my runs around potty stops.

Having done a whopping *three* races now, I arrived at the 10K race location feeling like a veteran. It was mildly amusing to see a few others who looked as unsure as I had felt at my first race only three months ago.

Paul and I picked up my packet and took it back to the car, where I pinned on my number. I noticed a course map inside the race packet. I made the mistake of looking at it. My "veteran" feelings vanished.

"Paul, look at this. The course winds up and down and around so many streets, I don't think I can cover that distance. In fact, this map makes the course look like a long *drive*."

"Don't worry, Bet. You can do it. What's that you've been telling me? Start out slow, and then just keep moving. If you don't stop, you have to make it to the finish."

But I didn't want to merely make it to the finish. I wanted a decent time. I knew I wouldn't place in my age group. Rose probably would; she was much faster than I was and consistently placed. Barbara might place, depending on how many women were in our age group. At the last race, I had finished only slightly behind Barbara, and I wanted today to be no different. But the distance looked *long*. And then there was Paul to impress. He had such confidence in me.

When the gun sounded, I glanced over to the side of the road to see Paul with his camera in his hands and expectation on his face. He gave me a "thumbs up" and snapped a picture. *I have to do this. I can't disappoint him—or me.*

As I got underway, I repeated Shane's words to me at the start of my first 5K, "Let the rabbits go." I concentrated on my breathing until I settled into a comfortable pace, a pace I thought I could maintain for a few miles. I had never stopped for water during a 5K before, but this time I stopped at the first aid station, at the two-mile mark. I walked briskly, just long enough to drink. When I started running again, I felt renewed energy. Then I was at three miles, and then four, where I stopped for water again. I still felt steady after five miles. Then the unimaginable happened. I actually passed people during the last mile. Not many, and I also got passed. But I passed enough people to convince me of the benefit of pacing.

Paul was at the finish line, snapping photographs. "Way to go, Bet! I knew you could do it." His face reflected the achievement I felt. His chest swelled as he gave me a hug.

Barbara and Rose both finished ahead of me. As expected, I *didn't* place in my age group. Rose placed second and Barbara third. I wasn't far behind Barbara, but finish order no longer seemed important. I felt great simply for having finished a 10K with enough strength to pass people near the end.

~ ~ ~

In December of that year, I ran another 5K, this one in conjunction with a half-marathon (13.1 miles). The half started at seven-thirty and the 5K started at eight. Because of the shorter distance, the 5K runners would all be in before the half-marathoners. About thirty minutes after I finished, the first of the half-ers started coming in.

Watching runners cross the finish line, I was astonished. "Paul, look at the first-place woman. Her time is an amazing one twenty-three." I tried to do the math in my head. *Thirteen miles in eighty-three minutes ...at six-minutes miles, the finish time would be seventy-eight minutes.* "She just ran an average pace of six-and-a-half-minute miles, and she did it for *thirteen* miles."

"Yeah, so what?" Paul looked at me with a puzzled look on his face. He didn't get it.

"This is discouraging. I only ran three miles and my pace was about an eight-and-a-half-minute mile." My shoulders slumped.

Paul put his arm around my shoulders. "That's all right. You're comparing yourself to the fastest and youngest runners in the area. Remember, you're way ahead of the majority of the population. Focus on that."

"Thanks, but I guess I'd better get to work if I want to be competitive. I can't run *one* mile at a much faster pace than I just ran three, and I couldn't run thirteen miles at any pace."

We remained at the finish line to cheer for Rose and Barbara, who were doing the half. They both looked strong when they came in.

We stayed for the awards ceremony for both events, which took place after the half marathon. The 5K awards were given out first. When my name was called for third place in my age group, Paul nudged me and said, "See there, Bet, you placed." He eagerly snapped pictures of me accepting the award, as if it was some great accomplishment.

I knew better.

When I got back to him, I said under my breath, "Thanks, but that's only because all the good runners did the half." I looked at the award. "So this doesn't really mean much."

Rose placed third in the half marathon. Barbara didn't place, but her time was good enough to make me envious.

I had begun to feel a tiny bit like a real runner, until that day brought my feet right down to the ground (pun intended). These people were *real* runners—the ones who ran faster and longer. I was a greenhorn, a neighborhood jogger. I'd never be able to run as far as thirteen miles. Even worse, I didn't think I'd ever be competitive in my age group. I had neither speed nor endurance.

Paul did his best to cheer me up during the drive home, but I was too busy wondering how to improve my training to pay much attention.

CHAPTER SEVEN

For the next several months, I found myself stopping at newsstands to look at running and fitness magazines. I subscribed to *Runner's World.* I dedicated Tuesdays and Thursdays to speed training, and continued to use the weekend run for distance. The speed workouts usually followed the plan described in the most recent article I'd read. I learned about fartleks, Swedish for "speed play," alternating intense effort with easy effort. The next article touted the benefits of track workouts, so I switched to running six to eight intense quarter miles with a cool-down in between. After I read an article that recommended timing full miles, *that* became my speed work. Then I tried running all three miles fast. One after the other, I changed to nearly every plan I read about. My training log showed improved times for my neighborhood treks, but I remained doubtful my effort would pay off in the next road race.

Meanwhile, Paul willingly tromped through dewy fields on chilly mornings, and waited patiently, camera in hand, at finish lines. When the logistics allowed, he stood on the side of the course and snapped pictures as I went by. "Looking strong, Bet. Keep it up."

Even though my 5K times *did* get a little faster, I slowly realized I didn't enjoy speed work. In fact, I started dreading each speed day. I'd gotten comfortable with five and six mile runs, because I could keep to a moderate pace. As for my speed, I decided to be content to just show up and finish. The small improvement in time wasn't worth the work required. Once in a while, depending on who showed up, I placed in my age group despite my unimpressive times.

While I stayed with my five-to-six mile long runs, I couldn't get the memory of the half-marathon out of my mind. Banter among runners before and after most races often included discussions of longer races. Barbara and Rose talked about doing the next Gasparilla Distance Classic in Tampa, a 15K (9.3 miles). I'd already heard from many local runners say it was a favorite. Runners discussed who was doing the next half marathon, and sometimes even

41

talked about doing full marathons. A full marathon was way beyond my grasp, but I started dreaming of running a half-marathon.

During that fall and winter, I had been getting to know Paul's daughters, and he had been getting to know mine. My daughters, much older than his, accepted Paul right away. I had been alone a long time and they wanted me to be happy with someone. If Paul made me happy, they were happy.

Paul's daughters were not so quick to accept me. Paul's divorce was more recent, his daughters were younger, and they weren't eager to see him with another woman. Paul didn't rush things, though, again saying, "I have the rest of my life." Ten-year-old Kathleen, mildly autistic, had apparently long been a daddy's girl, and tended to like whatever and whomever he did. Once she accepted something as "normal," she wanted it to remain that way. After her dad persuaded her that I was going to be a part of his life, she acknowledged that as the new normal.

Jennifer, fourteen, had defended her mother in the divorce. At the time, she felt somewhat distant toward her father, and she certainly wasn't enthusiastic about him dating. As the months went by, though, and the pain of the divorce lessened, even Jennifer became comfortable with our relationship.

By the spring of 1989, Paul and I were staying together nearly every night, either at my house or his apartment. One night while we were preparing dinner, Paul turned from the sink, where he was washing salad greens, and said, "I've been thinking, Bet. You're paying for your house and I'm paying for my apartment, but we're rarely using both places at the same time. How about we get a place together?"

I looked up from the stir-fry. I had been thinking along the same lines, but had been reluctant to bring up the subject. Logically, it made sense. "Our lives would be easier if we weren't going back and forth between two places."

"Much easier. No more wondering where I left my favorite blue shirt."

"But are you sure you're ready for that kind of commitment?"

"Yeah, I'm sure. I love you. I'm not going anywhere. I'm like an annoying gnat. In your face all the time." He made a buzzing sound as he moved his head in circles.

I laughed. "You're not annoying. It's just a big step."

"Here's big step for you." He pretended to swat at me with a dish towel.

42

"All right, I give up. Just don't hurt me. Yes, I'd like to live with you, Paul."

"Good. Then it's settled."

"You want to move in here?"

Neither of us gave serious consideration to me moving into his small apartment. I had a roomy, four-bedroom house. It never crossed our minds that I would give up my extra rooms, or a houseful of furniture. But Paul could fit easily into my house. Most of his furniture was rented, and he had few other personal belongings. His daughters could have the spare bedrooms when they visited. Paul had other ideas, though.

He wiped his hands on the dishtowel and slung it over his shoulder. "This is your house, Bet. When I stay here, I feel a bit like a guest. Not that you don't make me feel welcome, but I don't think I'd ever feel like this is *my* house, or *our* house. I'd always think of it as *your* house."

I looked at how comfortable he seemed to be in the kitchen, but then thought about how many times he asked where something belonged, or asked where something should go, or asked which drawer he could use. "Okay, then what do you want to do?"

"Why don't we choose a house together, one that will be ours?"

I stirred the vegetables and tofu once more, and then turned back to him. "Okay, I like that idea. And maybe I can keep this house, too. My dad always said real estate is the best long-term investment."

The next couple of weekends, we visited several open houses in the area. We didn't see anything we liked that was also affordable, but we talked to the realtor at each house, explaining what we were looking for.

A few days after the second weekend of looking, one realtor called back and said she had found several properties she thought we might like. She showed us eight houses, but none of them felt quite right. Then she said she had saved the best for last. She took us to a cute house that seemed to fit us from the first look. We both liked everything about it—the location, the layout, the colors, and even the price.

The feature we liked most was the screened back porch overlooking a small, shaded, secluded back yard. That porch became important in two ways. First, it was where Paul went to smoke. In the beginning, Paul seemed to think that if he simply blew the smoke away from me, it wouldn't bother me. But over time, he realized that no matter what he did, it did bother me. He had recently decided to not smoke in the house.

More importantly, though, the porch was where we spent many hours daydreaming and planning our future. We kept a second coffeemaker there, and spent many Saturday and Sunday mornings in the quietness, with the newspaper, the birds and squirrels, and our dreams.

~ ~ ~

Paul sat nestled in his corner of the back porch, between the table and the outside wall of our bedroom. I sat across from him. The coffeemaker and sugar bowl were nearly hidden by the many sections of the Sunday paper.

"Paul, do you think I could do a half marathon?" I let the crossword puzzle fall into my lap, and tapped the pencil on the arm of the chair.

He looked up, coffee mug in hand. "Sure you could. You'd just have to train for it. Remember when you didn't know if you could run six miles? And now it's no problem to go that distance."

"I don't know. I have a feeling that going from three to six was a lot easier than going from six to thirteen would be. I think I need to read about running longer distances. Want to go to the bookstore with me?"

"Have I ever turned down an opportunity to go to the bookstore? Maybe LeCarre's new book is out." He started folding the paper.

Paul was a voracious reader. His favorite authors included John LeCarre, Ken Follet, Tom Clancy, Robert Ludlum, and Len Deighton. He often got antsy waiting for the next spy thriller, resorting to reading books by what he considered "lesser" authors.

"I'm glad I didn't have to come over there and threaten you." I winked. "Let's go."

CHAPTER EIGHT

Never having spent time in the sports section of a bookstore, I was unprepared for the variety of books. Most of the books on running seemed to be directed to athletes competing on an advanced level. One after another included discussions of VO_2 uptake, target heart rate, and glycogen stores— none of which I understood. These books seemed to be directed to the young, elite athlete. That certainly wasn't me.

But then a title caught my eye. The cover of *Galloway's Book on Running* claimed it could teach almost anyone how to complete a marathon. From the description and the endorsements, it seemed to be aimed more at the "regular" runner, even a beginner, rather than the elite. Galloway's running credentials were sound. And he had been an ardent supporter of women's running.[4]

From reading *Runner's World,* I knew a little of the history of women's running. I had read about Kathrine Switzer running in the 1977 Boston Marathon as the first officially registered female. In 1978, women were still so new to marathoning, I thought it must have been courageous for Galloway to co-sponsor a marathon put on for women.

But as impressive as Galloway's biography was, two reasons to buy his book stood out. First, Galloway claimed that nearly anyone who could run three miles could complete a marathon by following his plan. He didn't expect his reader to be young, fast, or competitive, but wrote for the average runner.

---

[4] Jeff Galloway was a 1972 Olympian in the ten thousand meters. He trained with Frank Shorter, winner of the 1972 Olympic marathon, and Jack Bacheler, ranked in the top four in the world in the ten thousand meters from 1969 through 1972.

In the mid and late seventies, Galloway continued competing at long distances, and ran a 2:16 in the Houston-Tenneco Marathon. (The willing time of many marathons is over 2:20 and the men's world record at that time was Shorter's 2:10:30.)

Galloway co-founded the Avon International Women's Marathon in 1978.

Second, his training schedules called for only three runs a week. Since I was already running three days a week, this book seemed to be aimed at me.

Paul met me at the checkout with three new spy novels. We went home, settled in on the back porch with a fresh pot of coffee, and started reading.

Eager to know how to train for longer distances, I read every spare minute. Galloway had developed a fresh approach to endurance running, a philosophy surprisingly different from those I'd been reading in *Runner's World*.

First, he recommended less total weekly distance than most other coaches, emphasizing that rest days are training days, too. Even though the importance of recovery had long been recognized in sports such as bodybuilding—body builders rarely work the same muscle group two days in a row—most running coaches still advocated running daily. Galloway said that for the average runner, excessive weekly mileage needlessly increases the risk of injury. Since the benefit of a long run lasts for about three weeks, there is no reason to do them too frequently. He found the lower-mileage approach prepares runners for the endurance requirement of a marathon as well if not better than more miles.

The three-day-a-week plan called for two shorter, but more intense, runs during the week, and a long easy run on the weekend. I soon learned that the definition of "short" and "long" were relative terms. I considered my current six-mile distance long. Galloway's training schedule, after about eight weeks, labeled a *ten*-mile distance *short*. I couldn't imagine running ten miles at all, and I certainly couldn't grasp the idea of that being short. *What distance will be considered long?* I didn't want to know just yet; I was afraid to read that far. However, I was ready to get started on the first steps of the plan, which was to get to ten miles.

The plan was to add a mile to my long run each week, keeping the runs during the week the same distance I'd been doing. So I extended my next weekend run from six miles to seven. I didn't feel much difference, except a tiny thrill, as if I'd embarked on an adventure. *Will it be as easy to go eight next week? Can I build up to thirteen miles?*

The next week, I made it to eight miles, again adjusting my pace a bit slower. Nine miles was harder the next week—my knees and hips were sore in a way I hadn't felt before. And I got bored. At my slow pace, nine miles took a while. I had to work at occupying my mind for the last few miles. I hadn't run with a radio before, but thought it could help to get through runs that long. The next week, I bought my first Sony Walkman.

Because of the knee and hip tenderness I had felt on the nine-mile run, I didn't push as hard during my mid-week runs and decided to do a second nine-miler before increasing the distance again. The soreness wasn't as bad the second time; I hoped my body was adjusting to the stress of the longer distance. And the radio helped with the boredom. A third nine-miler couldn't hurt. This time the soreness was hardly noticeable.

Finally, it was time to attempt a major milestone—ten miles. For reasons long since forgotten, I scheduled it for a Friday evening. The announcement to several coworkers of my plan for the evening gave me added incentive. I had to do it then, to avoid the embarrassment of failure. One of the guys even brought me his homemade brownies for energy.

From my house, there were two one-mile loops that brought me back home, and a two-mile leg going south. From the far end of the two-mile leg, there was a three-mile loop. I started out along the familiar circuits, planning to piece together enough segments to make up the ten miles. At about three miles into the run, just as the light was fading, I stepped into what I thought was a puddle of water. It wasn't water. It was a pothole that caught my foot, bringing me down. Fortunately, I rolled out of the street and onto the grassy utility easement. A kind driver who saw me fall and stopped. "Are you all right? Do you need help?"

"I'm fine, thanks," I declared. He looked doubtful, but drove away. In truth, I really didn't know how I was because I refused to look. *If I look, it might hurt, but if I don't look, I won't feel anything. No matter what, I will complete this run.*

I brushed myself off, turned up the radio, and continued on my way. The endorphins must have been flowing, because I didn't feel much. Only some stinging and something warm trickling down my leg.

Seven triumphant miles later, I raised my sweat towel[5] in the air, and said to no one, "Yes!" When I reached the house, I finally looked at my knees and elbows. Yuck! Three streams of blood had run down my left leg and were now crusty. My left shoulder was scraped and bloody as well. Another dark trail ran from my shoulder down to my elbow. Minutes later, the necessary

---

[5] I had developed the habit of running with a small towel in my hand to wipe the sweat off my face, and wipe my drippy nose. It was also a great "rally" towel.

shower awakened nerve endings most unpleasantly, but the thrill of having finished ten miles pushed away most of the pain.

Now that I had reached the ten-mile mark, I read further and learned that ten miles was to be my base distance. From that point on, I'd add two miles every two weeks, keeping to the ten miles on the alternate weeks. Then after twenty miles, …well I wasn't sure I'd ever make it to twenty. (A typical training chart is in Appendix 1.)

Sticking to the training plan was made easier by Paul's encouragement. He had become an enthusiastic cheerleader for me and for many of my running friends. With his support, I was even more determined to complete a half marathon.

Meanwhile, the reading continued. I had purposefully paused each time I read about and then tried another bit of advice. "Turnover[6] contributes more to speed than stride length." I was skeptical about this concept when I read it. It didn't seem to me I could change the frequency of my steps much, but extending the distance covered with each step seemed an intuitive way to gain speed. But I experimented during races, and found Galloway was right. I matched my pace to a few other runners and then increased my stride length. For reasons I still don't understand, I couldn't maintain that level of effort for long without becoming too winded, so the net result was that even though I sped up initially, I soon slowed significantly. The other runners left me.

I tried quickening my turnover, and to my surprise, my pace increased with hardly any additional effort, and I was able to maintain the faster pace much longer.

Then I reached the most controversial part of the book, where Galloway talked about the walk break. He had discovered that runners who periodically slowed to a brisk walk for a minute extended the distance they were able to cover and also recovered faster. He recommended walking for a minute after each ten minutes of running. The endurance benefit of the long run wouldn't be diminished, and the risk of injury would be substantially reduced.

The idea of walking part of the distance raised a lot of controversy among marathon runners and trainers. On one side were the purists who said running meant *running*, not walking, and that it cheapened the competition of the marathon to include those who walk part of the distance. It helps to

---

[6] The speed of steps

remember that until the early 1990s, marathoning was considered by most people a sport for only a select few—those who were young, athletic, and naturally had the gift of endurance. This was no sport for ordinary people.

On the other side of the "walk break" controversy were those who contended that very few marathoners, or even half marathoners, run the entire distance without any stopping or walking. Only an elite few don't walk at the aid stations, and many others walk near the end, when they become too fatigued to run. The people in this camp felt that completing the distance, however one can do it, is worthwhile. I was decidedly in the second group. If I could finish thirteen miles, no matter how, I'd accept the finisher's medal with no shame.

After several more ten-milers, and with Paul's urging, I accepted Rose's and Barbara's invitation to go with them to the Gasparilla Distance Classic 15K in Tampa in February 1990. Very early on a Saturday morning, we rode together from Orlando to Tampa, found parking close to the start, and walked over to the packet pickup location. We pinned on our numbers, used the indoor bathroom (a treat for runners), and then returned our packets to the car. It was by now about twenty minutes until race time, time to make our way toward the start line.

We merged into the crush of runners heading to the start—more runners than I'd ever seen in one place. Never having been in a race that large, I was reminded of the apprehension I had felt at my first road race. I was again out of my league. Grateful for the company of Rose and Barbara, I tried to put that out of my mind as we jostled for a place in the start area.

"Let's try to find the back of the field," Barbara said.

"Yeah, I don't want to be trampled by the fast guys," Rose added.

"Fine with me," I said. We walked for about two blocks before entering the crowd.

"This race is so big that we won't start moving until several minutes after the gun," Barbara explained.

Sure enough, it took us about four minutes to reach the *start* line, a first for me.

We all three stayed together for the first mile and a half, when Rose pulled away. I wasn't surprised, since she was the fastest. Then two miles later, Barbara looked over. "Are you all right with this pace?"

"Yeah, but I can tell you're able to go faster than this. Go ahead."

"Are you sure you don't mind?"

"Of course not. Go run your race."

"Just stay with a comfortable pace. You'll do fine."

I did just that, while trying to monitor my speed, respiration rate, and heart rate. I wanted to stay within a "conversational" pace. I'd read a great description of a conversational pace—you can talk if you need to, but you'd rather not. At each water table, I walked while I drank. (I've never mastered the art of drinking while running, or even while walking *very* fast.)

As I pulled away from the last water table at about eight miles, I started pushing harder. Knowing I had barely more than a mile, I picked up the pace as much as I thought I could maintain. Rounding a corner, I saw the finish line come into view. A wave of excitement washed over me. I pushed even harder, and crossed the finish line at a near sprint. Having a medal hung around my neck in the finish chute was thrilling—this was my first race in which every finisher received a medal. I met up with Rose and Barbara and discovered that I had finished only a few minutes behind Barbara.

We walked to a nearby restaurant and enjoyed a hearty breakfast—all wearing our medals proudly. Mine didn't come off until I was back at home. I even took it to work the next week to show it off. I had run a 15K!

CHAPTER NINE

Even though I had my sights set on a half-marathon, Galloway's advice on training for a full marathon was becoming more fascinating. Many articles advocated training runs no longer than twenty miles, but as many as two to three each week. Galloway disagreed, instead recommending runs up to the full twenty-six miles, but fewer of them. To complete a twenty-six-mile event, train up to that distance. Because the benefit of a long run lasts up to three weeks, one need only do distances longer than twenty every two to three weeks. This keeps the average weekly distance minimal, and thus decreases chances of overuse injuries.

The argument was all very logical, although I couldn't yet envision *myself* running distances that long or that often.

In late September, when the weather started to cool a bit, it was time to get serious about the half marathon coming up in December. I had done several 5K's recently, which had interrupted my weekend long runs. I used Galloway's plan as a model, but adjusted the distances down to get back to ten. Still thinking of ten miles as a long run, I alternated between my base of six and longer distances. Six, then seven, another six, then eight, another six, then nine. And so it went through eleven and twelve. Then it was the week to do thirteen. Even though at the outset of the run, I felt less anxiety than I had felt the first time I tackled ten miles, a vibration went through me as I approached the end of the route. I was a half marathoner—almost. (Technically speaking, I hadn't tacked that last tenth onto the end.)

Still, my spirits soared briefly—until the realization set in that I had merely covered the distance. I hadn't done it under race conditions, and I had been slow. I increased my every-other-week six-mile run to seven, just as insurance. There was something about "more than half" that seemed to have merit.

The December race morning finally arrived, cool and clear, and brought with it a sudden plunge in confidence.

As we drove to the race location, I retied my shoes a couple of times, and said little.

"You seem nervous," Paul commented.

"Yeah, I am." My voice was uncharacteristically quiet.

"Why? You've already done several fourteen-mile runs. This is only thirteen."

"But not in a crowd of other runners, and not with the temptation to go too fast in the beginning. I just hope I can make it all the way."

"Don't worry, Bet. You're ready for this."

We picked up my race packet, and I pinned on my number. I looked around at the crowd of runners. This event drew a much larger field than our shorter races, nearly as many as Gasparilla.

I intended to line up near the back, but shortly before the start, some friends dragged me farther up toward the front. They said we'd lose too much time if we stayed so far back. When the gun went off, I tried to look upbeat while I smiled and waved at Paul on the street. He was such a natural cheerleader that he looked as if he expected me to win or something. If only I felt that ebullient.

I tried to keep to my own plan, but I was surrounded by enthusiastic, faster people. I kept telling myself *slow down, take it easy*, but it was hard to listen to that voice amid the field of runners jockeying for position, whooping in excitement, and yelling "Come on. Pick it up." By the end of the first mile, my split time told me I had started out too fast. *Uh-oh. Will I have enough left for the end?*

At the first water stop, just two miles into the race, I walked long enough to drink. Most of the runners didn't stop for water—many surged ahead. With so many people streaming by, I wondered if the "walk break" plan would work for a race. But when I started running again, I felt refreshed and I slowly gained on some of the runners who had passed me. *Could this be another benefit of the walk break?* The same thing happened at the next water stop, and the next. The result was that I was still surrounded by many of the people I had been near since the early miles.

Between ten and eleven miles, something unexpected happened. Some of the runners who had started out fast in the beginning were now barely moving, either walking or running slowly, while many of those who had started out with a steady pace remained steady. I was grateful to be in the "steady" group, and I passed a few of those who had been the rabbits in the beginning. I just hoped my turn to crash wasn't lurking around the next corner.

Several long inclines greeted us between miles eleven and thirteen. Unprepared for the hardest part of the course to come at the end, I used the same tactic I used during training: I shortened my stride and concentrated on a quicker turnover. I breathed deliberately, fighting the urge to pant, instead breathing deeply and holding the air just a moment before releasing it.

After the last incline leveled off, I could see the finish about a quarter mile ahead. The voice of the race announcer reached out to me and pulled me in. I even had enough strength to speed up just a bit at the finish, and crossed the banner with arms raised in triumph. I finished a half-marathon! It was only a year ago that it seemed impossible to run thirteen miles, and now I had done it! Not only that, but my time was better than expected—two hours, five minutes. I had anticipated a time closer to two and a half hours.

By the time Paul found me emerging from the chute, tears were trickling down my face. "You did it, Bet! You looked so strong coming in." With a big smile and even bigger hug, he seemed as proud as if he had run with me. He took several pictures of me with the finisher's medal hanging from my neck and the finish line in the background.

"Thanks. Did you see my time?"

"Yes, I did. I'm glad I didn't listen to you and came to the finish sooner than you said. I had a feeling you'd be faster than you expected." He didn't even seem bothered that my sweat had gotten him wet. I think he considered us a race team.

"And the best part is how many people I passed in the last few miles. I think the walk breaks really helped me stay on pace." I felt so proud, I couldn't stop gushing.

"Now do you believe me when I say you should consider doing a full marathon?" Paul asked as he put his arm around my shoulder.

"Ha! In your dreams. There's no way I could go back out there and do that whole thing again," I replied. We walked toward the water table.

"Well, I remember when you weren't sure you could do a 10K, then a 15K, and here you are a half-marathoner. You really should think about it."

In fact, I didn't think about it much for a few months. After the half marathon, I ran my way into 1992, occasionally setting a new PR (personal record) for the 5K or 10K. Paul continued going with me to most races, wishing me well at the start, and waiting for me at the finish, camera in hand.

He asked me about my times after most training runs. He wisecracked about my calloused feet, my sweaty clothes, and the number of age group awards that were starting to clutter the house. And, of course, he kept making jokes about how he could inspire me to run faster.

With an impish grin, he told me to pretend I had just stolen something valuable and the cops were chasing me. His blue eyes twinkling, he said to imagine ten thousand bucks waiting for me if I set a new PR. Sometimes, just remembering one of his jokes during a race made me chuckle to myself. This relaxed me so much that I ran more efficiently. Indirectly, his inspiration worked.

While most runners enjoy getting age-group awards, very few runners are serious enough to go to extremes. One older man I knew tried to improve his time by bringing a diver's air tank with him to road races. He had the tank filled with an oxygen-rich mixture. Just before the start, he went to his car and breathed this mixture for a few minutes. I couldn't imagine the effect lasted more than a minute or two, but he expected it to give him an edge. After the race, he was furious that he didn't win in his age group. He muttered, "I need to enrich the mixture more next time. I know I can beat those guys."

Most runners, though, are content to rely on their training and natural ability, and happily root for other runners, even those in the same age group.

I never considered measures as extreme as the oxygen mixture trick, but I did try some of the visualization techniques described in Galloway's book. One chapter is devoted to harnessing the power of the mind to affect the body's performance. One suggestion is to spot a runner ahead that you want to catch. Then imagine looping a large rubber band over that runner, and feel the rubber band pull you closer to the runner.

Another one is to visualize helium-filled balloons attached to your wrists and ankles, combined with a tail-wind, so that the overall effect is the sense of being simultaneously lifted and pushed forward.

I used each of these, sometimes with remarkable results. In one 10K, I imagined large, bright red balloons attached to my wrists, ankles, and shoulders. I gave myself a tail wind, and felt the lifting force the entire way. I set a PR that day. I even beat Barbara a few times, although I never got close to Rose's times. She was so fast that I knew it would take more than visualization to be ahead of her. And I had already concluded that serious speed work wasn't for me.

In April of 1992, I brought the mail in and was sorting through it on the kitchen counter. Paul was sitting at the kitchen table with a mug of coffee and a spy novel.

"Hey, Paul, look at this."

"What is it?"

"Track Shack's starting a marathon training program, and guess whose training method they're going to use?" I nodded my head toward the coffee table where Galloway's book lay.

With raised eyebrows, he said, "Galloway's?"

"Clever man, you are." I sat at the table and showed him the flyer. "I don't think I'd be able to do a full marathon, but I want to go to the organizational meeting. I'm too curious about the program to miss hearing about it."

"But you could, if you wanted." He looked over his mug at me almost as if he were daring me.

"Could what?"

"Could do a full marathon."

"Uh, I'm not sure about that. But I'd like to train with other runners."

CHAPTER TEN

About forty runners attended the meeting to introduce the marathon training program, including a surprising number of people my age. I was forty-eight and a few people looked to be in their fifties or older. Betsy Hughes, co-owner of Track Shack, spoke first. "I attempted several marathons before I finally finished one. I even went with my husband and my mother to England for the London Marathon. I fully expected to finish that one with sheer determination. But I didn't. Like the other times, I seemed to 'hit the wall,' and was forced to drop out."

I've never dropped out of an event, but then I've never tried to run a full marathon, either. And if Betsy, an experienced runner, found marathons so difficult, what are the chances of me doing one? Not so good. After hearing that, I thought it even more *unlikely* I'd do a marathon, but I still wanted to know more about how the training group would work.

Betsy continued, "Then I bought Jeff Galloway's book on marathon training. I was skeptical at first. I know some of you might be skeptical, too, if you've heard about his methods, especially the part about the walk breaks." She paused, and then continued with emphasis. "But I tried the plan and *it worked*. Not only did I finish, but with a time faster than I had hoped for. All of the parts of the plan—the gradual increase in mileage, the walk break, the slower pace—it all worked for me.

"Some of you might know that Jeff is starting training programs in several cities around the country. We contacted him about helping us set up a program here because we want you to have the same success I had."

After hearing a little more about Betsy's experience, I decided to sign up, if only for the opportunity to train with other runners. I still didn't plan to do a marathon, but I could train for another half, using the Galloway method with other runners.

We were to meet each Sunday morning for a long run, beginning with a distance of six miles. The first week, our runs were to be timed so that we could be matched with others who ran at similar speeds and put into pace groups.

Forty-six of us met at the north end of Central Park in Winter Park for the first Sunday run together. Some people looked chipper and eager to get going, while others looked barely awake. We reminded each other to be quiet; not everyone in the area might appreciate a loud group of people at six in the morning.

Mike Bourque, the trainer for the program, greeted us. "Good morning, runners. Here are maps of the course we'll run this morning." He passed around small maps of the route. "Remember not to go out too fast. We'll be timing you, but that doesn't mean this is a race. We want to know your speed for a normal training run that includes the walk breaks. By next week, we'll have you divided into small sub-groups according to your paces. Have a good run, everyone."

Planning to follow the Galloway method of alternating ten minutes of running and one minute of walking, we set our count-down timers for ten minutes and off we went.

Because of our differing speeds, the faster runners surged ahead and the slower runners fell behind. I found myself with three others whose pace was close to mine—Martha Christopher, Tammy Gappen, and Russ Barkett. We weren't the slowest group, but we were definitely in the slower half.

Russ, whose age I judged to be close to mine, was the most experienced distance runner, having done a couple of marathons already. His graying hair and olive skin gave him a distinguished look, even in running shorts and singlet. "I'm here because I don't like to do long runs alone. I need the motivation and the entertainment, so I expect to hear some great stories, ladies." His wife was in the program for walkers preparing for a half marathon.

"I've never done a marathon," said Martha, "but my husband James and I have decided this is the year. He's here, too, but in a faster group. Today's six miles matches my longest run ever. I'm trusting in this Galloway approach." In her early thirties, Martha's strong body propelled her swiftly enough that she often placed in her age group in 5Ks and 10Ks. Her dark, straight hair seemed to match her mental strength; she had complete confidence she would finish a marathon.

Tammy, in her twenties, was small, with curly, sandy-colored hair. "I've only been running for a couple of years, and I've only done a few 5Ks and one 10K. But I want to run one marathon, just to say I've done it." Because of her youth and slight build, I expected her to be faster than the rest of us, but that was not the case. She was the only one for whom we occasionally slowed. At forty-eight, I was proud to be able to maintain the same pace as these younger women.

I chimed in with my reasoning for being there, "I don't really expect to do a full marathon, but I want to train with you to learn more about distance running, and to be able to extend my longest run."

The four of us stayed together throughout the course and decided we were so well matched that we'd like to run together from then on.

We were not surprised the next week to find that we were placed in the same pace group. We ran a comfortable seven miles, made easier because of the walk breaks. Martha found the breaks awkward at first, saying that it was too hard to start back running. Tammy tended to walk too slowly. I liked the walk breaks from the start, though. After only a few weeks, it was apparent that the walk breaks made it easier to complete the distance and left me feeling better afterward. Over time, as the length of the runs increased, all of us looked forward to the beeping watch that signaled us to walk.

Our usual course included a few hills, at least by Florida standards. Of course, *hill* is a relative term, like *long*—defined by one's point of view and experience. Martha encouraged us to "charge" the hills. She had learned that the best way to make it up a hill without stopping was to shorten her stride, but quicken her pace and lean forward slightly. We came to depend on her rally cry of "Charge!" each time we approached a hill.

Every few weeks, a clinic was presented on a topic such as shoe selection, stretching, nutrition, running form, etc. During the clinic on nutrition, we were told that as we increased our distance, we'd need to take in some kind of energy food during a run. Many of us had never run far enough to require energy food, so we had no experience with products such as energy bars and energy gels. We were advised that the training runs were the time to experiment. We'd learn when, what, and how much.

When the distance reached fourteen miles, I wasn't concerned about completing it, because I'd already run that far. I made it through, although toward the end I slowed a bit more than expected. Two weeks later came sixteen. I was uneasy for two reasons. First, it would represent a new milestone, which nearly always made me a little nervous. Second, it was now in the heat of summer. Regardless of how early we started, it was going to be hot and humid. I finished the sixteen, but felt lightheaded during the last two miles, which caused me to go *much* slower. Remembering the clinic on nutrition, I realized I must need to eat something during a run over fourteen miles.

The week before we did eighteen miles, I shopped for PowerBars. I started nibbling on one at mile eight and finished it over the next four miles. I finished the eighteen-mile run feeling better than I had at the end of sixteen. The PowerBar made the difference.

Meanwhile, Mike, the trainer, had been watching us as we ran so that he could advise us on our form. He pointed out that I tended to swing my hands across my body, with my elbows sticking out on each side. This caused my upper body to twist too much. *So I guess I don't have the form of Joan Benoit after all.*

He said my hands should move only backward and forward, parallel to my body's movement, and my elbows should stay tucked in near my sides. To prevent my shoulders from twisting, I should imagine a rigid steel rod running through both shoulders.

These changes weren't easy. It's hard to change the way we do something as natural as running. I got into the habit of doing a "form check" each time I started running again after a walk break. Eventually, Mike noticed improvement, even when I was not thinking about it consciously. I noticed that I ran with slightly less effort, and also that my clothes didn't chafe as much. Less rotation meant less friction.

With the increase in distance, I was learning how important it was to select clothing carefully to minimize chafing. What is negligible for a shorter distance gets magnified at longer distances. I classified my shorts and bras into "short run only" and "long run" groups.

Still unsure about doing a full marathon, but having completed eighteen miles, I went out for twenty miles two weeks later. With the help of a PowerBar and Martha's "Charge!" I did it. When I got back home, Paul had the coffee ready on the back porch as usual.

"How did it go?" he asked.

"I made it, and feeling okay, too." I sipped the coffee Paul had handed me. He always knew just how I liked it.

Paul nodded his head and pursed his lips. "You really should do the marathon with your group, you know." The marathon the group was planning to do was the Jacksonville Marathon in January of 1993.

"Well...I'm starting to think about it." I couldn't suppress a half smile, a little smug that I had just finished a twenty-mile run.

"If I had an application, I'd send it in for you."

"Is that a threat?"

"You might take it that way." He winked and smoothed his mustache. "Seriously, I think you should do Jacksonville with your group."

The next week, I stopped by Track Shack to get an application. I was in my office when I filled it out. *I can't believe I'm registering for a marathon.* My hand trembled and I fumbled the pen twice as I filled it out. I hoped the bank didn't inspect the signature on my check closely; it was a little shaky. As I sealed the envelope, I thought, *no turning back now.*

Mike told us that it's natural to have bad days and good days, so we shouldn't be upset if some of the runs didn't go well. Many athletes will agree that most days are normal. Some days the body simply doesn't want to comply with our demands; but there are those few rare days that seem magical, when everything works exceptionally well.

The day I attempted my first twenty-six mile run, I remembered Mike's guidance. It was the last long run before Jacksonville. I'd been pleased and surprised to complete twenty-three miles just three weeks before, even though the last three miles were not easy. But this was the big test. If I could get through this, I'd be ready for the marathon. I started out as usual with Martha, Tammy, Russ, and a couple more. Somewhere around mile eighteen, Russ and I lagged behind the others. It was very hot, so I blamed my difficulty on the conditions. We plodded on through twenty-one miles, trying to maintain our run-walk ratio. But for the next mile, light-headedness forced us to walk more and run less. After another mile, we could hardly run at all.

Apparently, when Martha and Tammy got back to the park where we started, well ahead of us, they reported that Russ and I were struggling. Russ's wife Toni, who was waiting for him, drove the course until she found us about three miles out and gave us cold Gatorade. (I still count her among my angels.) The Gatorade was refreshing, but still not enough to get us running.

"I'm sorry if I'm slowing you down, Russ. Each time I try to run, I get short of breath, as if I'm oxygen deprived. I felt lightheaded and my stomach is queasy."

"You're not slowing me down at all. I've been afraid I was holding you back. I feel pretty much the same as you."

"My body simply doesn't want to run anymore. I don't understand what's going on, but I'm going to have to walk it in."

"I agree. Let's try to walk as fast as we can, though."

But we didn't walk "fast." We straggled back to the park feeling discouraged and a little embarrassed because we were the last ones to make it in. I don't remember how long the run took us that day, but I remember that it took nearly an hour longer than we had hoped.

Mike told us not to worry. He reminded us about good days and bad days. He said, "Just think about it this way. Today, you got your bad day out of the way. Three weeks from today will be your good day."

When I got home and went to the back porch where I knew Paul was waiting with the coffee, I dreaded giving him the report.

"Well, did you run a marathon today?"

I looked down. "No, not really," I answered meekly. "Russ and I had a hard time. We mostly walked the last three miles. After today, I'm not sure I can do a marathon."

"Don't worry about it, Bet. You'll do all right on race day."

"I hope so."

Why is he so confident? I don't feel confident at all.

CHAPTER ELEVEN

On the second Saturday in January, 1993, Paul and I drove to Jacksonville. After checking into our hotel, we joined a group of other runners in our training group, along with their spouses and friends, for a pre-marathon dinner. For most of us, this was our first marathon. We talked over strategy, wished each other a good run, and agreed to meet at the race location the next morning at seven-fifteen for the eight o'clock start. We all headed off to an early bedtime, though few of us expected to sleep soundly.

I awoke with a start several times during the night, heart racing from a bad dream. In one, I overslept and missed the start. In another, I lost my shoes. In yet another, I was moving through molasses. Each time, I sat up abruptly, and Paul assured me that everything was all right and that it wasn't time to get up yet. When the alarm finally *did* beep, I was sleeping soundly for the first time. Startled, I jumped up quickly and looked around the unfamiliar room, trying to remember where I was. It took several seconds for me to remember, "Oh, this is the big day."

The night before, I had laid out my race clothes, and all the other items I'd need: energy bar, lubricant, sunscreen, race number, etc. After dressing quickly and going through my pre-race preparations, I turned to Paul, who wasn't fully dressed yet, and impatiently announced, "I'm ready. Let's go."

"But it's only six thirty," Paul said.

"I know, but I'm nervous. I'd rather go early. We don't know about parking, and I'm too antsy to stay here. Please hurry."

"Okay, I'll be ready in a sec," Paul said, as he slowly shook his head and sighed. He quickly finished dressing, and grabbed a cup of coffee and his camera bag.

It was a good thing we left early, because traffic was congested and we had to search for a parking spot.

The temperature was nice—in the fifties, with overcast skies and a high of seventy. Close to perfect. In the start area, I lubricated my feet, underarms, and chest—again. I drank an energy drink, went to the bathroom a couple of times, and met up with most of the Orlando runners. Russ, Tammy, Martha and I planned to start together, and hoped to finish together.

About seven forty-five, Russ said, "It's time to move out to the start line."

"Okay, I'm heading for the back," said Tammy. I agreed with her.

Martha and Russ disagreed. "We'll lose too much time in the back. Let's go to the middle."

Tammy and I gave each other a look, shrugged, and followed.

Paul stood on the side of the road, and took my warm-ups, along with Martha's and Tammy's. With only a few minutes to go, he gave me one last hug for good luck. The pre-race announcements were brief, and then we heard The Star Spangled Banner, after which the field of runners inched forward into a tight knot.

Emotion that I still can't explain rose up from my core and warmed my cheeks. After the months of training, the time had come. I fought back tears as the announcer counted down to the start. "Ten, nine, eight, …"

BOOM! With a blast of the air horn, we were off.

It's finally here. This is it.

The combination of the build-up, the anthem, and the air horn brought a second wave of sentiment. My eyes welled up. I looked around to see if I was the only one dabbing my eyes, and was relieved to see others doing the same.

We were barely able to walk at first, but soon we were able to run. The tears dried soon after we were moving at a normal pace, although I still felt a surge of excitement every few seconds.

"Let's remember to keep our normal pace," Tammy reminded us.

"I'm depending you to hold me back so I won't go out too fast," Martha added.

"Yes, we have a lot of miles ahead of us. We shouldn't get too excited this early," I added.

Somehow, we lost Russ in the first mile, but Martha, Tammy, and I were still together. We jockeyed for position, passing slower runners and walkers, but trying to stay to one side when it was time for our walk breaks so that we wouldn't impede anyone else. Even though we tried to stay within our plan, it was hard to settle into a comfortable pace.

The first few miles slipped by easily. We worried that they were too easy. At a water stop around mile five, Martha pulled ahead of Tammy and me. This didn't surprise us because we knew Martha was naturally faster than we were. The field of runners continued to spread out, and soon few others were near us. Tammy looked over at me. "Hey, Bettie, there's the eight-mile marker already. How do you feel?"

"I still feel good. I can't believe we're at eight already." I felt more comfortable than I remembered ever feeling after eight miles.

"Me, either. I just need to remember how many miles we have to go."

"I agree. If I start to go too fast, be sure to tell me to slow down." I remembered what we had heard at one of the clinics, that a marathon is an energy management competition. I wanted to hold myself in check during the early miles.

At mile ten, we again remarked how good we felt.

Then we were approaching the split for the half-marathoners. "Wow, here's the half coming up. Still feeling good?" I asked Tammy.

"Yeah, I do. I'll probably pull back my pace just a little, but I'm still feeling all right."

"No problem. I'll be happy to slow down with you." I wasn't out for time anyway, and I enjoyed Tammy's company, so I didn't mind slowing a tad to stay with her.

At mile fifteen, I turned to Tammy. "I feel like I've finally found that perfect pace. I know I can't, but at the moment I feel as if I could just keep going like this forever."

"Well, if we never see you again, we'll know you couldn't stop," laughed Tammy.

Between sixteen and seventeen, Tammy began to slow more, so that I got a little ahead of her. When I realized I was a good thirty feet ahead, I did an about-face and went back.

When I got nearly back to her, she said, "Bettie, you're going the wrong way."

"I know. I'm coming back to you."

"Go, Bettie, go. This is your race. You don't have to slow down to stay with me."

"Are you sure? I don't want to leave you."

"Yes, I'm sure. I'm slowing more now. I can't keep up with you. Go."

Reluctant at first, I moved ahead of her, trying to maintain a comfortable pace and keep from going too fast. My time at mile eighteen was three hours, five minutes. I tried to do the math in my head, to figure out what pace I was on. My brain was too tired to do the calculations, but I knew that was faster than I had expected. *I can definitely finish this in less than five hours. Can I make it in four forty-five?*

I tried to slow a bit, afraid I was going too fast with eight miles to go. But it seemed just as hard to go slower as to go faster; apparently, I had only one pace. The mile markers were still coming to meet me as steadily now as they had in the beginning.

As I neared mile twenty-one, my thoughts went back to the last long run just three weeks earlier. *I just can't have a meltdown like I had that day, or worse. I'd be so embarrassed if I couldn't finish.* I realized I had to push all negative thoughts away. *Remember, Mike said this would be a good day.*

Luckily, that's when I spotted Paul ahead on the side of the road. We hadn't known beforehand if he would be able to come out on the course, so it surprised me to see him. Because I was doing so well, I was energized as I ran over to him. "Give me a hug for luck," I said, not caring how sweaty I got him.

He gave me a brief hug, a quick kiss, and a cold Gatorade. "You're on a fast pace, Bet. Don't overdo it."

"I know. I'm trying to be careful, but I'm feeling so good." I waved my sweat towel in the air as I left him.

Nearing the twenty-two mile marker, I felt a shiver of excitement run through me. *Take it easy, you've still got four miles to go.*

By mile twenty-three, my pace slowed a little, but I still felt tons stronger than I had at that point had just three weeks prior. Also, I realized I had been passing runners who were walking or barely running. Each time I went by another one, I felt a little more energized.

At about a half mile from the finish, the course left the paved road and wound through a wooded area that led to the back side of a stadium. The finish line was about two-thirds around the track. After I entered the wooded area, the grass and dirt slowed me—I even walked a bit. When I emerged from the trees and was able to see the entry to the stadium, I also saw that earlier finishers and spectators were greeting each runner as he entered the track. A surge of energy coursed through me.

I entered the track holding my hands up in victory, and waving my sweat towel. The end was right around the far end of the track! I couldn't make out the digits on the clock, but I felt like a celebrity as cheers greeted me.

"Go, Bettie." I looked over to see Russ and Martha. They had already finished and were there to cheer in the rest of us.

I made my way down the straightaway and approached the turn. As I came around the end of the track, I put my hands up again. Then I saw the clock. It read 4:28! I had broken four and a half hours! This was beyond my wildest dream.

I saw Paul snapping photos as I entered the finish chute. By this time, tears were flowing again. A jumble of emotions welled up as my chest swelled with pride.

I continued to the end of the finish chute, where I was given a finisher's award and a bottle of water. At the end of the chute, Paul scooped me up and spun me around. "You did it, Bet! Great run. How do you feel?"

"I'm on cloud nine. I just finished a marathon." I couldn't stop smiling.

"And you were so worried after your last long run."

"Mike's prediction was correct. There are good days and bad days. Today was a magic day. Everything worked."

"And you broke four thirty. You didn't think you'd do that, did you?"

"No, I was just hoping to break five."

I gingerly moved on down the track in search of food, clutching Paul's arm. The after-race snacks included hot chicken soup. The slight breeze on my wet clothes had started cooling me down already and the soup was just what I needed. Paul, seeing I was getting cold, dug into the gear bag for my warm-up jacket and put it around my shoulders.

We walked over to where a few other Orlando runners were and sat to watch more finishers come into the stadium. Conversations buzzed around us.

One guy frowned as he said, "What's this stupid thing?" He held up the Lucite finisher's award. "I wouldn't have done this one if I'd known there wasn't going be a medal!"

Someone else chimed in. "Yeah. How can I hang this thing around my neck?"

Since this was my first marathon, I didn't understand the significance of their disappointment at not receiving a medal. I thought the stand-up plaque was just fine. It said I had finished a marathon. That was good enough for me.

"Why's everybody so upset about not getting a medal?" I asked the group.

"For most marathoners, it's all about collecting those medals," explained a man. "For a marathon, finishing is all most of can expect. So the finisher's medal is important."

Just then, we spotted Tammy coming out of the wooded area and onto the track.

Paul helped me to my feet and we headed back to the finish line to meet her. "How do you feel, Bet?"

"I'm cold, my feet hurt, my legs hurt—and I've never felt better." A broad smile erupted on my face. "I broke four thirty!" I still couldn't believe it.

We reached the finish line about the same time Tammy did.

"Yay, Tammy, good job," I yelled.

She didn't speak, but waved as she walked through the finish chute and collected her finisher's award. At the end of the chute, still breathing hard and obviously spent, she managed to smile. "I'm glad it's over. At least I finished in under five hours." I glanced up at the clock. It read 4:49. "What was your time? You looked strong when you left me."

"Four twenty-eight."

"You broke four thirty! None of us expected to be that fast. I walked a lot after you left, but it looks like you didn't."

"I stayed pretty steady. I passed a lot of people in the last couple of miles."

"Good job."

We each grabbed a bottle of water and walked toward the food tent. I was certainly tired, but elated that the run had gone so well.

The overall winning times that day for the first man and first woman were probably under three hours, and several people I knew were under four hours. All along, I expected to be in the back of the pack. Even those of us bringing up the rear take some pride in how we rank among the last runners, though, and since I was primarily concerned with just finishing, the better-than-expected time was what people back home call *lagniappe*[7].

During the drive home that afternoon, my mind wandered back to conversations with Barbara and Rose, my two friends from local road races.

"Paul, how do you suppose I was faster than either Barbara or Rose? They've run a few marathons, but have never broken five hours. And yet, I can't beat either of them at short distances."

"I don't know. Maybe you trained better than they did."

"Maybe. I remember reading an article in *Runner's World* that talked about why some people are good sprinters, but no so good at endurance, while others are the opposite."

---

[7] Lagniappe is a French term used primarily in Louisiana and means "a little something extra" or an unexpected benefit.

"Yeah, what did it say?"

"I remember something about muscle fibers being either slow-twitch or fast-twitch. I think it said that some people have a lot more of one kind."

"What's the difference in slow and fast?"

"Slow-twitch fibers give you better endurance and fast-twitch fibers give you more speed. Maybe Rose and Barbara have more fast-twitch fibers than I do, which makes them better at the shorter distances. I must have plenty of slow-twitch fibers."

"And your slow-twitch fibers just broke four thirty."

"Yes, I did! Who would have thought I would complete a marathon, and under four and a half hours? I wish my PE teacher could see me now."

"You deserve to be proud, Bet. You'll be qualifying for Boston[8] before long."

"I doubt that. I'd have to knock off another forty minutes. I'm not interested in working that hard."

I leaned back and put my feet up on the dashboard. I couldn't stop smiling.

---

[8] The Boston Marathon is the only major marathon that requires runners to run a qualifying time. At the time, the qualifying time for my age group was 3:50.

CHAPTER TWELVE

It wasn't that I didn't enjoy the satisfaction of having completed the Jacksonville Marathon, or that I wasn't proud of my time. The glow soon faded, though, leaving me feeling flat, kind of like the week after Christmas. I needed a new goal.

Following Mike's advice, I cut back on my mileage to allow a full recovery from the marathon. Also, since the race marked the end of the training program, there would be no more group runs on Sundays for the next few months. I decided to try once more to improve my short race times. This meant returning to speed work. Although I already knew I didn't enjoy this as much as distance running, I needed to focus on a challenge. So back to the track I went.

Generous soul that he was, Paul offered to help me with my speed. "I'll bring my pellet gun out to the next race. Every time I see you, I'll just fire at your rear end. That'll make you speed up."

Not that I was ungrateful for such a motivating plan, but it would take more than his threats to improve my times. I made friends with the stopwatch. Some days, I timed the second mile of a four-mile run, using the first mile for a warm-up. Other days, I resurrected the fartlek approach, which meant that after a mile warm-up, I alternated between speed bursts and slowing enough to catch my breath. My times for the measured miles inched downward, so that I consistently ran under eight minutes. While an eight-minute might not sound impressive to most runners, it was significantly better than I had been running.

That spring, I ran nearly every 5K in Central Florida. The speed work paid off, and I placed in my age group more often. The collection of race awards grew. Noticing this, Paul surprised me by installing three shelves on the family room wall, dedicated to my ribbons and trophies.

Two significant things happened that spring. First, Paul created a job for himself. Having been laid off several months earlier, he listened with intense interest as I described growing problems at work. I was the lead software engineer on a small contract, reporting to the program manager. The program manager was overloaded and was leaving some important tasks undone. He was a competent engineer, but not so interested in some of the managerial and customer relations aspects of the contract.

Paul realized these were the very tasks at which he excelled. He went in to see the chief operations officer, and offered to work for half-salary for three months as a trial. At the end of that period, the company would have the option of either letting him go or bringing him on at full salary and with full benefits.

After only a few weeks, the management's appreciation was obvious, and we knew he would be offered the job permanently. No one was surprised when the offer was made well before the end of the three months.

The second thing was that Paul occasionally joined me on easy runs. No one could have been more surprised when he announced, "Watching you, hearing about your problems, and seeing your progress has piqued my interest. I need to experience this for myself."

So he started out by coming with me for my first, warm-up mile, which I ran even more slowly when he was with me.

"Okay, I'll admit it's harder than it looks," he said, after some huffing and puffing. Of course, he hadn't given up his beloved cigarettes, so it was no surprise that he got winded easily.

Having him along forced me to go slower, but always made it more fun because he kept me laughing. At the same time, I tried to hide my pride in knowing I could easily run much faster and much longer than he could. Each time he turned back for home and I switched to my normal pace, I nearly felt like Joan Benoit again. I tried to remain humble, but some days it was hard.

Paul gasped for air. "Hey, slow down...a little...will you?"

We were just warming up. I thought we were going pretty slow. "I'm sorry. I thought you said this is *easy*."

"Well, it *looks* easy. But I see what you mean about your lungs being your limiting factor. And remember, I'm just starting out. You've been at this a lot longer."

"But you're the one with a heart like a horse, remember?"

Paul, when discussing his smoking, always quoted his doctor, who had once told him that he had a strong heart, a heart like a horse. "Yeah, and right now, it's working like a horse." He wiped sweat from his forehead.

"Okay, I'll ease up on you. But only if you admit that this running stuff is harder than it looks. And promise me that at the next race you won't stand near the finish line and yell to me, 'Just speed up' as if it's easy." I couldn't hold back a crooked smile.

"All right, all right. I get the message. Now let's go slower, or else you're going to be carrying my collapsed body back home."

In May, the marathon training program started up again. I was eager to get back to the Sunday runs. Although I had maintained speed drills during the week, I had not kept up the weekly long runs. The target event for the group that year was the Marine Corps Marathon in Washington, D.C., scheduled for mid-October. Paul and I were excited about visiting the city, and I was ready to prove to myself that I could run a "real" marathon. Jacksonville, with its relatively small field, seemed more like a local event, while the Marine Corps was a large, nationally known—and well-respected—event.

On the Sunday of the first group run, I returned home to find Paul in his usual place on the back porch with a fresh pot of coffee.

"Well, how did it go?" He poured coffee for me and stirred in exactly the right amount of sugar.

I put my feet up on an empty chair. "I was disappointed that it was less organized than last year."

"Yeah, how?"

"First, they told everyone they only needed to be able to run two miles to join the program, but we began with a five-mile run."

"So there could have been people there who had not run any longer than two miles?" Paul frowned.

"Exactly. Several people said they weren't prepared for five miles." I raised two fingers. "And second, there were no course maps, so the new people had to depend on those of us who ran last year."

"But what if they couldn't keep up? Did they just get lost?" Paul tugged on his mustache while he looked into the back yard, a sure sign he was thinking hard.

"Some did, apparently. A couple of us veterans hung back and looked for people who looked lost. We found one guy, Scott, straggling by himself. When we asked him if he was a member of the group, he sighed, 'I'm trying to be.' He had been promised that the first run would be only three miles and that there would be groups at all paces. But even the slowest of the other runners had gone ahead, leaving him lost."

"Poor guy. Why did he join the group?"

"He wants to continue to lose weight. He's already lost about seventy-five pounds, but he's still heavy. He said he wants to do the Disney Marathon in January as a way to celebrate his success. We slowed down a lot and stopped for extra walk breaks to help him get back to the park."

Paul nodded while he listened, smoothing his mustache and looking into the sky beyond the backyard. I could tell he was turning something over in his mind.

I waited, unsure what he was thinking.

Then he suddenly looked over with a sparkle in his eyes. "You know, Bet, I've never wanted to run long distances. And I certainly don't intend to run a marathon. But your program needs a new pace group—a group for people like Scott. I bet he's not the only one who would like a group that goes very slow, maybe takes more walk breaks. Do you think the program director would let me lead a group like that?"

"What? You would do that?" My jaw must have dropped. I never expected to see Paul take part in a running program.

Paul raised his eyebrows. "Surprised?"

"Yes. More than surprised, I'm shocked."

"Well, like I said, I don't want to actually run a marathon. Hell, I've never wanted to run even a 5K. But I certainly know what it's like to be slower than everyone else. I'm the one lagging behind every time I run with you. I'll join that program if I can form a group for people like Scott—and me. And I won't have any problem taking more walk breaks. You think Mike would let me?"

"I think so. He looked overwhelmed by the end of the run today. He's a fast runner himself, and I don't think he knows what to do with the very slow people. I think Scott would be grateful for you, too."

Paul joined the program to lead a new group—about seven runners and fast walkers. Most in his group, like him, intended to do just a half marathon, so they built up the distance more gradually than the other groups. Nevertheless, they were out there getting in the miles.

74

Every time I heard him telling someone at work that he was in a running program, I was amazed all over again. Some thought he wasn't serious. Mr. Meat-and-potatoes, smoker, no-exercise guy was actually running!

Several weeks after he joined the program, we were cleaning up after dinner. Paul wiped his hands on a dish towel and slung it over his shoulder. He leaned against the counter. In a contemplative voice, he said, "You know, Bet, I'm probably happier than I've ever been in my life. When I wasn't working, I loathed feeling unneeded. But now I have a job I like—one I created for myself. In fact, this may be the most rewarding job I've ever had."

"I've notice that you're relaxed lately."

"And I have you, and now I'm even learning to like running. Life is good. What more could I want?"

I hooked my arm into his. "I feel the same way. Everything about our lives is good. The kids are all doing fine. We both have good jobs. We enjoy this home. I'm lucky to have you." I stood back and winked at him. "You know, I kissed a lot of frogs before I found you."

"Whoa, hold on. Who found whom?"

"Okay, okay. You found me."

He put his arm around my shoulder. "You bet I did. And I'm not letting you go, either."

CHAPTER THIRTEEN

Until he began running with the marathon training group, Paul had run in old, nearly worn-out shorts and t-shirts. Now that he was around other people, he needed better running clothes.

Meanwhile, I had started wearing a cap when I ran. Caps were useful, regardless of the situation. In the sun, it shielded my eyes. In rain, the bill kept the rain off my face. The cap also served as a sweatband, and it kept my hair out of my face. I had been wearing whatever I could find, which were mostly heavy cotton caps. I wanted a lightweight cap, one better for running.

We went to a local sporting goods store to shop for both of us.

After we had selected shorts and shirts for Paul, I looked for caps. From the Day-Glo colors that were popular then—mostly pink, orange, and green—I happened to choose pink. Bright pink.

The next Sunday, several other runners joked that the pink cap had been lighting the way. Others remarked that the bright cap made it easy to keep me in sight. As the weeks wore on, members of my group asked me to always wear the pink hat because they could recognize me—even from a distance.

I still participated in most of the local races, now always wearing the pink hat. More and more people noticed its bright color, and I became known to many runners as "the lady in the pink hat."

The week my group reached a distance of eighteen miles, Paul's group ran eight. He got up that morning eager to meet the road. "This is my big day, Bet. My group's going eight today. I know that doesn't impress you, but it's a big deal for me and my group. By the way, don't forget your PowerBar. You're going to need it today."

Paul finished his run much sooner than I, and waited at the park for me to come in. He had been done long enough that his clothes were almost

77

dry, but he still looked tired and sluggish, as if he'd just finished. I didn't say anything, although I was a bit odd.

On the drive home, I said, "I feel much better than I did last time. The energy bar really helped. How did your eight go?"

"I finished it, but it was much tougher than I expected. It took all I had to keep going for the last mile."

"Sorry it was so tough."

"Of course, I've never run eight miles before, so maybe this is what it feels like. If this is normal, then I *know* I can never do the distances you do."

"Going eight was hard for me the first time, too, and I had a much more solid base."

"Maybe it's this cold that's sapping my strength. I wish I could shake it. Just when I think it's gone, it seems to come back. I feel wiped out. I'm going back to bed when we get home."

I'd forgotten he'd been fighting sniffles off and on for a couple of weeks. *He must be feeling really bad out if he's skipping coffee on the back porch.*

Paul remained unusually tired for the rest of the day. I tried to remember if my first eight-mile run had affected me as much. It hadn't, but then I'd been running for years already.

We had a major design review that week at work, which meant we were to be in day-long meetings every day. He didn't say much about how he felt on Monday and Tuesday, but he was more subdued than normal. On Wednesday afternoon, Paul slipped me a note. "Feel worse. Think I have fever. Going to the 24-hr clinic after work."

I looked at him carefully and realized he hadn't said anything for quite a while, which was uncommon for him. Normally, he would be quipping one-liners frequently. His face was drawn and his shoulders slouched; he looked exhausted and he had little color in his face. I was surprised I hadn't noticed sooner just *how* bad he looked. My focus had been too much on the meeting and too little on him.

Paul was not one to see a doctor over something minor. His decision to go to a clinic told me he believed he was sick with something more serious than a cold. Two hours later, I understood why his run had been so hard and why he had continued to feel so bad. He didn't simply have a cold—he had pneumonia! Little wonder it had been hard for him to run eight miles. The doctor started him on antibiotics and ordered more tests.

A few days later, we were even more shocked to find out he had *both* bacterial and viral pneumonia. The doctor cautioned Paul that it would take a long time to fully recover, and that he would need to stay on the antibiotics for at least three weeks. He suggested Paul come back then for a follow-up X-ray.

Paul decided to skip his Sunday runs until he felt completely well, but he saw no reason for me not to stay on track with my own training.

"You'll have to run for both of us for awhile, at least until I can shake this pneumonia."

Perhaps it was because I increased my distance faster this time, or maybe it was because I was in different shoes, but I had blister problems for the first time. After trying different brands of lubricant, I settled on Bag Balm. Developed for dairy farmers to use on cows' udders, Bag Balm has been used by nursing mothers for years. It contains lanolin, which maintains its lubricating capacity longer than most other products, including many that claim they're formulated specifically for runners.

"How are the blisters, Bet?" Paul asked from his chair on the back porch. He wasn't one to stay in bed, and he was feeling a little stronger.

"Still there. The Bag Balm is good, but doesn't solve the problem completely when I go more than twenty."

"I heard an ad for something called NuSkin. It's painted on like nail polish and used to cover and protect minor cuts and scrapes. I wonder if that would help."

"Can't hurt to try it. Seems like I've tried everything else."

For the next long run, I applied two coats of NuSkin the night before, giving it plenty of time to dry, and then I used Bag Balm on top of that.

The combination worked surprisingly well.

Weeks dragged by and Paul still wasn't back to normal. My anxiety about him escalated. He had gone back for a follow-up X-ray, and this one revealed a dark spot remaining in his right lung. The doctor said it looked like a stubborn spot of the infection, or maybe scar tissue, either from this illness or from another event earlier in his life. The doctor didn't seem worried about it, but suggested to Paul that if he wanted peace of mind, he should have a CAT scan.

The company had made Paul a full-time employee, but the start of his medical insurance coverage was still a few weeks away. When he found out how much a CAT scan would cost—he was quoted a thousand dollars—he decided he could wait until his insurance would pick up the tab. After all, the doctor didn't indicate a sense of urgency to have the test.

Even after his cough was nearly gone, he couldn't seem to get his energy back. Regardless of how much he rest he got, he felt fatigued most of the time. Since he hadn't been able to gather the energy to run again, he found someone to take over his group. We both realized that whatever was draining his strength wasn't going away easily.

In early September, Sophie, a pulmonary therapist in my pace group, asked how Paul was doing since his pneumonia.

"He's better, but not back to normal. He can't get seem to get his energy back."

She thought a moment, frowning. "Sounds like something else is going on. He could have allergies or something else chronic. He should see a pulmonary specialist. I can recommend a couple of doctors." She wrote down two names when we got back to the park.

On the back porch, I passed along Sophie's message.

"I've felt bad long enough. Since my insurance is now active, I think I'll take her advice," Paul said. His insurance had become effective in the previous week.

I had expected more resistance. *He must be feeling even worse than he's letting on.*

A week later we sat in the office of Dr. Lawrence Gilliard, a pulmonologist. He looked at the films we brought with us. Like doctors often do, he started with, "Hmm." A moment later, he said, "Well, I see a dark mass here. Hard to tell exactly what it is from the film. It could be from allergies, or an old scar, or something else. I recommend both a CAT scan and a bronchoscopy so we can get a better look at what's going on. But it's probably nothing too serious. You said you had pneumonia recently. Maybe it's from that."

"What's a bronchoscopy?" Paul asked.

"We run a scope down your trachea and into the bronchial tubes so that we can look at the tissue. That'll give us a better idea what we have here."

Paul coughed nervously, and then asked, "Is it painful?"

"We'll sedate you so you won't feel a thing."

"Well, then let's do it. I want to know what's wrong with me. I haven't felt good for a long time now." At that point, Paul almost seemed a little excited. Again, I could tell he was eager to get healthy again.

Dr. Gilliard made the necessary phone calls to arrange both procedures while we were still sitting in his office. He didn't give me the impression that it was need, but I noticed he didn't waste any time, either.

After we left Dr. Gilliard's office, I was worried, but I didn't want to reveal my anxiety to Paul. I didn't ask him outright what he thought. His mood vacillated between deep thought and delivering his usual one-liners. It was difficult to gauge the degree of Paul's anxiety.

Two days later, before dawn, we checked in at outpatient services for the bronchoscopy. We were taken to a small, curtained-off cubicle containing only a bed and a tiny bedside stand. Paul was given a hospital gown, and asked to change. He fidgeted and coughed nervously, uncharacteristic for him. With nothing on but the gown, he complained he was chilly, except for his feet. Unlike me, his feet were the warmest part of his body. He tried to be humorous, but most of his quips were lame by his standards. For the first time, his eyes revealed unmistakable concern.

The CAT scan had been performed the afternoon before, but that wasn't invasive and he seemed relaxed as he lay on the table. This morning was different.

"I'm nervous, Bet. Stay here until they come for me." He reached out and grasped my hand. Just then, a nurse came in and gave him a sedative, which made him nearly unconscious by the time I was shuffled off to the nearest waiting room.

Once installed in the small waiting room, my apprehension spiked. I had been trying to stay strong and calm while I was with Paul, but now, sitting alone in the quiet, fear of the possible results gripped me. The invasiveness of the procedure and the sight of him looking so helpless on the gurney made me face the possibility that we could hear bad news.

The issue of *Runner's World* that I had brought failed to penetrate my brain. There was an article on blisters that I had looked forward to reading, but the words didn't register. I tried to watch TV, but couldn't follow whatever program was on. The mental image of Paul's worried look when the nurse explained the procedure kept flashing before my eyes. *Maybe it was just the procedure itself that had him worried. After all, I wouldn't want to have a tube put down my throat, either. Will it be an allergy or fungal infection, as Sophie suggested? Or could it be related to those damn cigarettes?*

Since I had known Paul, there was a small but certain fear that his smoking would someday have dire consequences. I tried my hardest to keep that thought buried, as if allowing the idea to surface would make it true. But my efforts were futile, and that fear seemed determined to find its way into my consciousness.

I wanted to pace, because that's what I do when nervous, but the room was too small. So I fidgeted and prayed.

Oh, God, please don't let this be the thing I dread the most. It's taken so long for us to find each other, please don't take him away from me now.

Soon after we started dating, Paul made a remark that I had forgotten until then. One day out of the blue—I don't remember what the topic was—he commented that he wouldn't live past fifty. At the time, I reacted as if he were teasing, jesting something along the lines of, no, you can't leave, or I'll come haunt you for all eternity. But now I couldn't help wondering if he had sensed something way back then.

CHAPTER FOURTEEN

Finally, the doctor appeared in the doorway. I didn't know Dr. Gilliard well enough to be familiar with his facial expressions, but I'd rarely seen a more somber look on anyone's face. He hesitated before speaking, as if he were trying to decide what to say. He took a deep breath, and then the words gushed out. "The dark spot we saw in the X-ray is a tumor sitting on Paul's right bronchial tube. We took both a brush biopsy and a needle biopsy. We should have the results in a few days."

The floor fell away like an out-of-control elevator. I couldn't find air. I sank into a chair as I struggled to find words. "Do you think it's malignant?"

Dr. Gilliard sat in the chair beside me. "We won't know for sure until we get the lab results. If it's malignant, there's a good chance it's treatable with chemotherapy or radiation. I'll refer you to an oncologist."

Oncologist? Did he just say Paul has cancer? I must have stared blankly. After a moment, he said, "Paul will be coming out of the anesthesia soon, and you'll probably want to be there when he does. I'll be in later to talk to him."

I mumbled something, but I can't say what. Thoughts flew about so fast, I couldn't sort them out. *This is my fault. I've warned him what his cigarettes would do, and now my prediction has come true. I made this happen. I'd rather have been wrong. What will we do?*

Suddenly I knew I needed to stay in the moment. I didn't have the luxury of looking beyond the next few days, or even the next few hours. After three deep breaths, I squared my shoulders, gathered my things, and returned to his cubicle. I didn't want to risk him waking up alone. I needn't have worried, though, because he was still unconscious when he was wheeled in a few minutes later.

I took his warm hand and whispered, "Oh, my dear Paul, nothing can happen to you. I simply won't let it."

About twenty minutes later, a nurse looked in on him, and said I needed to get him dressed so he could leave. *Does she have no compassion? Doesn't she know the test results? I refuse to rush him. What can she do?*

All I could get from him at first was incoherent moaning, but he finally started to mumble. "Where am I? What's happening, Bet?"

"You've had the bronchoscopy. It's all over."

"Oh, yeah. What did they find?" His eyes refused to stay open, his lids still heavy from the anesthesia.

Now, what do I say? How do I tell him that he has a tumor in his chest. But I knew what I had to say—the truth. We had never withheld anything from each other before, and I didn't think this was the time to start. "The doctor said he found a mass on your right bronchial tube."

"What does that mean?" His words were slow and a little slurred.

"He's coming in soon to talk to you." *Well, I didn't lie. Just didn't tell the whole truth. Better it comes from the doctor.*

Paul didn't process that explanation, though—too much sedative remained in his system.

Dr. Gilliard suddenly appeared and went to Paul's side. He picked up one of Paul's hands and said, "The procedure went well. It's all over."

"It's over?" He tried to raise his head and focus on the doctor's face, but couldn't quite make it.

"Yes. We found a mass on your right bronchial tube. We biopsied some tissue. We should have the results in a few days. We'll talk more then."

"Good. I'll see you then." Paul smiled. The lilt in his voice sounded as if he'd just made a play date.

I waited until he could sit up and focus his eyes before I helped him get dressed. When I judged him to be stable while standing, we started walking slowly toward the car.

Once in the car, his head began to clear. "What did the doctor say? I barely remember him saying something about a mass."

Dr. Gilliard must have known Paul wasn't lucid when he talked to him. Now it would be me after all who would have to clarify the message. "Yes, he said you have a tumor on your right bronchial tube."

"A tumor. That sounds serious." This time there was no smile. He grabbed the door handle, as if for support.

My fingers tightly gripped the steering wheel. I hadn't started the car. "He sent biopsy tissues to the lab, and should have the results by next Tuesday. We'll go back then."

"But he must have said more than that."

"The tumor is sitting on your right bronchial tube, nearly blocking it. He said you should see an oncologist."

"Oncologist," Paul repeated. The word hung in the air. Paul stared straight ahead and frowned. Sounds of passing traffic suddenly seemed to intensify.

All the air went out of me. I gripped the wheel tighter.

Paul said quietly, "Then it's cancer."

I couldn't lie to him. "It sounds that way."

He looked straight ahead and, after a moment, nodded his head slowly. "No wonder I had a hard time with eight miles. I not only had pneumonia, but only partial use of my right lung. At least I know why I've been so tired."

We were both shocked into silence for a few moments.

Paul turned and looked at me with searching eyes. "Did he say how bad it is? What my chances are?"

"No, he wouldn't even confirm it's malignant, even though he suggested seeing an oncologist."

We returned to silent mode. Paul looked away from me, out the window. I couldn't see his face. *What is he thinking? What would I be thinking?*

He looked back over toward me. He nodded slightly, as if in resignation.

What should I say? Should I try to console him? I had no idea what to say. I couldn't imagine what I'd want anyone to say to me if I were in that situation because I couldn't fathom what it would be like to receive that kind of news.

In spite of all my effort, tears ran down my face. For the second time that day, thoughts battled each other and I couldn't sort them out. I reached for a Kleenex. Paul patted my hand. "It's okay, Bet. Whatever this is, we're in it together." I looked at the wet streaks on his cheeks. *He's the one trying to make* me *feel better? That's backwards.*

"I know, Paul. You'll be all right." I only hoped I sounded convincing.

85

We were each locked in our own thoughts as I finally started the car and began the long, silent drive.

Once at home, Paul went to the back porch to smoke.

I let out an exasperated sigh and stared at him in disbelief. "Paul, how can you light a cigarette when you've just found out you probably have lung cancer? Can't you see those things are killing you?" With so many emotions roiling, I could feel my cheeks getting hot, unable to squelch my hatred of the cigarettes and my anger at his smoking.

"One more isn't going to make any difference now." He looked away from me.

I knew he was right, and I knew that the stress would make any smoker want a cigarette, but I couldn't control my fury. Better to leave. I went inside and busied myself for a few minutes before I was calm enough to return to the porch.

I tried to control my voice. "Look, Paul, I'm sorry about what I said. I'm sorry about the tumor and I'm sorry I got angry. But I *am* angry." My voice escalated in both pitch and volume, in spite of my best effort to manage it. "I'm angry that you have a tumor in your chest. I'm angry that you've been smoking those nasty cigarettes all your life." My lips quivered as I tried to hold back tears.

"Look, Bet, I'm angry, too. It's not fair. Just when my life is better than ever, this happens. But getting angry isn't going to help anything."

How can he be so calm? How would I react if it were me? The truth was, I had no idea how I'd react. "I suppose I should say something profound now. I should tell you something inspirational. But I have nothing."

Paul nodded slowly. "I'm numb right now. I'll wait for the test results, then I'll decide what to do. If it *is* cancer, I'll find out everything I can about cancer treatments. I'll find out more about alternative treatments, too. I'll fight it with everything I've got. I'm not ready to die."

Watching him look out into the backyard, my anger faded, and I suddenly realized that it was actually fear, not anger, coursing through my veins. Fear of losing him. I reached across the small table and clasped his hand. My voice little more than a whisper, I said, "Well, whatever you decide, I'll be with you."

"I know you will." Paul forced a small smile as he finished his cigarette.

86

On Tuesday, we were back in Dr. Gilliard's office listening to his description of the malignancy. The tests showed the tumor to be squamous cell carcinoma. In Dr. Gilliard's words, "garden variety smoker's lung cancer."

"Can you operate to remove it?" Paul asked.

"No, we can't. Because of its location. It's wrapped around your right bronchial tube, closing it off about ninety percent. And it extends behind the trachea."

My eyes met Paul's. Both of us registered shock. Not only had Paul run eight miles with pneumonia, but with lungs limited by both smoking and a nearly-blocked bronchial tube. We had been prepared to hear bad news, but this was even more severe than we had expected.

"What are my options?"

"I don't treat cancer myself. I'm going to refer you to both a general oncologist and a radiation oncologist. First you'll see a general oncologist who will oversee your treatment. Then you'll have an appointment with a radiation oncologist, who'll be responsible for the radiation therapy."

If Dr. Gilliard said anything else, I didn't hear it—I was dazed. I had thought I was prepared to hear bad news, but hearing the words spoken aloud was staggering.

That afternoon, we were in the second doctor's office of the day. Dr. Smith hardly looked up from Paul's file when we entered the room. He mumbled something about when he could schedule the start of treatment. Before he said much, though, Paul interrupted with a question. "Dr. Smith, before we talk about treatment, can you tell me more about the tumor? All I know is that it's squamous cell carcinoma, and it's on the right bronchial tube."

"I can only tell you what's in this report. Mmm, yes, squamous cell carcinoma. Lymph glands between the lungs are involved." He said it so casually he might just as well have been reading the weather report on a fair day.

Lymph glands. Just when I thought the news couldn't get worse, it did. Based on my limited knowledge, I thought that meant the cancer had already started traveling, which, as far as I knew, spelled tragedy. I forced my hands to be calm, although my mind was reeling.

Paul spoke first. "I didn't know about the lymph glands. Does that mean that it's spread?"

"Not necessarily. I see you're scheduled to have a bone scan. If it has spread, that should find it."

Paul seemed to be thinking over that news. He looked as though he was handling the information better than I was. But then I was busy trying to hide my reaction. I wondered if he was making just as great an effort to hide his. *What's really going on inside his head?*

Paul went right to the tough question. "With what you know now, what would you say my chances are?"

Dr. Smith ignored the question and continued as if Paul hadn't said anything, naming the chemotherapy drugs he would use, and saying Paul would need to spend two days in the hospital twice a week. Still looking down, talking more to the chart than to Paul, he nearly mumbled when he said, "I want to get you started on both chemotherapy and radiation right away. If we can shrink the tumor enough, then we can operate."

Paul tried another question. "What would be the effects of the chemotherapy?"

"As you've probably heard, the chemo will likely make you pretty sick, and you'll lose your hair. We'll give you something for the nausea, but you probably won't feel very good in between treatments."

Paul smiled weakly and attempted a joke—losing his hair would make it easier for him to fend off the women. It was awkward. He looked out the window for a couple of beats and then appeared to switch emotional gears. "So I couldn't work?"

"No, you probably couldn't." Dr. Smith remained buried in Paul's file, jotting down notes, as he spoke.

"What if I decide against chemotherapy?"

"Then you could have just the radiation."

"What are my chances with only the radiation?"

Dr. Smith finally raised his head and looked directly at Paul, but his eyes were empty. "The radiation will likely be the more effective of the two. Chemo isn't as helpful with your cell type as it is with small cell carcinomas, but it's still worth trying." He directed his attention back to the file.

"If I have only the radiation, can I still work?"

"Some people can keep going while getting radiation. It depends somewhat on the dosage and the frequency. That'll be up to your radiation oncologist."

Paul said with some determination, "It's important that I'm able to work. I'm going to pass on the chemo and go for only the radiation."

At that moment, Dr. Smith stiffened his back, turned away, and closed Paul's file. He had lost the modicum of interest he had shown initially. In response to Paul's questions about support groups and other supporting therapies, he mumbled "no" or "I don't know" or shook his head, and finally stood as a signal he was finished.

In the hall outside the office, Paul vowed, "Did you see how he wanted us gone as soon as I declined the chemo? When he knew he couldn't sell me his drugs, he had no interest in me. I hope I never have to never speak to that 'chemo salesman' again." Paul was so offended that months would pass before he agreed to see another general oncologist.

CHAPTER FIFTEEN

Dr. David Gerstley's genuineness was a welcome contrast to Dr. Smith's. He welcomed Paul with a warm handshake and a big smile. As he showed Paul the CAT scan films, he calmly explained the exact location and size of the tumor. It was about five centimeters wide and eight centimeter tall—much larger than I expected. It sat on the right bronchial tube, with tendrils wrapping around the bronchial tube and also around the trachea. The films made it clear why surgery wasn't an option.

"What are my chances?" Paul decided to try again to get an opinion.

Dr. Gerstley looked him right in the eye, and said quietly, "According to the statistics, less than thirty percent." But then he sucked in a breath and said emphatically, "But you're not a statistic. You can be in that thirty percent."

"At last, a straight answer. Thanks, doc. I intend to fight this with everything I can."

"Good. That's what I like to hear. Now we need to go over a couple of things. I'd like to start you on aggressive radiation therapy, which might have more pronounced side effects than you would hope. In order to radiate the tumor, the esophagus will get radiated, too. Eating will become painful, but I'll give you medications to help."

"Whatever you want, doc. I'm ready for it." Paul sat up straighter, as if he had rediscovered his courage.

Late that afternoon, in his chair on the porch, Paul was still trying to come to terms with all we had heard, both discouraging and encouraging. It had been hard to hear the pessimistic statistics, but then Dr. Gerstley seemed optimistic about the treatment efficacy. Meanwhile, I hungered for the right words to comfort him—and me. *What can I say to someone who has just been shown something inside him that will probably kill him?*

Paul looked puzzled. "I need time to think about my options. Tell me again about the guy who healed his cancer with the macrobiotic diet."

I repeated a story I'd told him soon after we met, about a doctor at Methodist Hospital in Philadelphia, Dr. Anthony Sattilarro, diagnosed with bone cancer, who healed himself by abandoning conventional treatment in favor of following the macrobiotic diet. Soon after he switched to the diet, his severe pain left him, and in six months his oncologist reported that the cancer appeared to be in remission. Two years later, he was declared cancer free. He wrote about his experiences in his book *Recalled by Life*.

Paul listened intently, then asked, "Now, tell me again about how this diet would work."

"Well, you know that it's a vegetarian diet, but it's more specific than that. You'd need to see a practitioner to have a diet prescribed explicitly for you."

Paul looked out into the backyard, intently focused on the birds sitting on the birdbath. Then he frowned as he looked back at me. "But you know what I like to eat, Bet. Even if I fully believed in its power to heal, I just don't think I could stick to a diet like that. I'll have to rely on something else."

"Do you have anything in mind?"

"Yeah, meditation to start. It worked with you, didn't it?"

Paul had told me how he used to sit in his office and visualize that I would be as drawn to him as he was to me. He truly believed that had played a big role in his gaining my affection. I was less convinced than he was. I still believed it was his humor—and the way he took care of me when I was sick.

He went on, musing more to himself than to me. "In addition to meditation, I'll learn as much as I can about other alternatives. There must be more options out there."

Over the next several weeks, in addition to the aggressive radiation therapy, he tried several other remedies. We started reading everything we could find. We talked with friends who had battled cancer. Upon the recommendation of one friend, he drank Barley Green. When that didn't seem to do anything, he followed the advice of another and drank diluted hydrogen peroxide. It was supposed to "super-oxygenate" his system, thus enabling it to fight the cancer. He even tried Essiac tea, obtained from a local spiritual/alternative bookstore. It was formulated by Rene Caisse, a nurse practitioner in Canada, and based on Native American remedies.

The effect of the radiation wasn't bad for the first couple of weeks, but just as we had been told, the effect was cumulative. Soon he was working shorter days, too fatigued to stay the full day.

Meanwhile, Paul talked with both Kathleen and Jennifer. By this time, Kathleen had been living with us for a nearly a year. Because she was mildly autistic, it was hard to gauge just how much she understood. She didn't appear to be greatly concerned, but we never knew for certain. Jennifer, who lived nearby, had reestablished a close relationship with her dad over the last couple of years. She seemed confident he would survive this, saying she just couldn't lose him now.

Through all this, Paul insisted I keep up with my marathon training and also insisted he still go with me to Washington for the Marine Corps Marathon. Dr. Gerstley not only gave him permission for the trip, but strongly encouraged him to go. He believed the diversion would give Paul a psychological and emotional lift that would outweigh any possible negative affect, maintaining that a short break in the radiation treatment would not diminish its efficacy.

We arrived in Washington on Thursday, planning to do our sightseeing on Friday and Saturday before the marathon on Sunday. Our hotel was in Crystal City, about a half-mile from the nearest metro stop. We tried to take it easy, although Paul wanted to take in as much as we could while we had the chance. He had a keen interest in history and politics, so he was eager to be the consummate tourist. And he wanted to prove he wasn't an invalid—not yet. I worried that he was over-tiring himself, but he wouldn't slow down.

Our hotel promised Sunday morning transportation to the marathon start/finish location for the many entrants staying there. We were told to be in the lobby at six thirty, and that a shuttle would take us to the race location for the nine o'clock start. When we entered the lobby ten minutes early, we joined the growing number of runners, which soon approached three dozen. But no shuttle. Then we learned the disheartening news that the shuttle buses were small, each holding only about eight people. As seven o'clock approached, a few runners called for taxis. We were about to do the same thing, until we heard that the taxis weren't promising pickups any time soon.

We then decided to do what most of the other runners were doing— we walked the half-mile to the nearest Metro stop. Paul insisted on carrying his camera, lenses, and monopod; the walk was a great effort for him. Then we had another half-mile walk from the Metro to the race start. It was so late I had to forgo a last bathroom stop. I was trying to apply lubricant while we walked. We reached the start area less than ten minutes before nine.

I was still fretting about the lack of a shuttle for several reasons. The most obvious was the inconvenience and the stress of having to get to start on our own. I also worried that the trek was too much exertion for Paul. And, finally, I thought there was no chance I would meet up with any of the runners I knew. About twenty-five runners in our local training program had traveled to D.C. for the marathon, and I had hoped to arrive at the start area in time to meet up with some of them. We had planned to run all or part of the marathon together. But in that regard, providence was on my side. As I worked my way into the crowd of sixteen thousand runners, I happened on a group of eight people from Orlando, including Russ, my old training partner.

I barely had time to look back and wave to Paul before the gun sounded. The number of people nearly overwhelmed me—nothing but runners as far as I could see in either direction. We soon spread out, though, as a result of the variations in pace.

The course took us by the Lincoln Memorial twice. The first time I approached the spot on the corner where Paul said he would be, I was stunned by the size of the crowd. Spectators were five and six deep on both sides of the course. *How can I possibly find anyone in that throng?* But he saw me. He said my bright pink hat made it easy to pick me out of the crowd. I stopped for a quick hug.

"How do you feel?" His shoulders sagged and his eyes looked tired.

"I'm fine," he insisted, although his voice sounded weak.

Later, when the course went by the other side of the memorial, I again looked for him. This was the last time we expected to see each other on the course. I slowed and looked hard, but didn't see him. I tried not to worry about him, but I feared the day had been too much for him. Part of me wanted to drop out and go see about him, but where would I look? The only reasonable thing to do was keep running and meet at the end as planned. I was so worried about Paul, I hardly noticed my time.

The course turned off Jefferson Davis Highway and entered Arlington National Cemetery. Because runners were required to run over a curb, a board had been placed there to create a ramp. As we approached the ramp, a course monitor said, "The finish is just around the corner."

This is an announcement well-known in marathoning circles as one of the top ten things runners don't want to hear because it's usually not true. To most of us, "just round the corner" should mean less than a tenth of a mile, but spectators are notorious for saying this as much as two miles from the finish. At this event, runners are destined to hear the same thing at least three more times, each time disappointed when there is no finish "just around the corner." The actual finish does not come until after several more twists—and more than a half mile.

That day, though, I was so new to marathoning that I naively believed the statement, so I tried to charge up the incline in front of me, expecting to see the finish soon. It wasn't that I was trying for time, but because I was focused on finding Paul. With burning lungs, I rounded the next turn only to see that the end was *not* in sight as promised. My labored breathing and screaming legs forced me to slow. I approached the next turn expecting to see the finish line—but again, no finish in sight. Runners around me were grumbling loudly, "Where is it?" Finally, we made one more turn and saw the large banner.

At the finish, each runner was given a medal by a marine in full dress uniform, and then guided along a predetermined path that led eventually to the reunion area. Because the field of participants was so large, proceeding along this route was slow. When I finally reached the reunion area, I looked and looked for Paul, but couldn't spot him. I saw two others from Orlando who said they had seen him earlier, and he didn't look well.

We should have stayed home. This was a mistake. I should have known this trip would be too much for him.

Then I saw him. He was leaning on a small pylon and his face had a grayish tint. He brightened when he saw me and picked up his shoulders. "Hey, Bet. Congratulations." He tried to be cheerful.

"Thanks. How are you, Paul? You don't look good."

"I'm just a little tired. I'll be all right."

I took his camera bag and we leaned on each other as we walked slowly to the Metro stop. Once on the train, he breathed deeper and regained a bit of color. "I just got a little overheated and thirsty. I'll be okay when we get back to the hotel."

I handed him my water bottle. *I didn't even think about where he would find something to eat and drink while I was running.*

~ ~ ~

After we both had a shower and a nap, Paul's color looked a little better and he seemed somewhat recharged. I wanted to believe him when he said he felt fine, but I also knew he was operating with diminished lung function. He had probably worked much harder than I had during the marathon. Guilt hit me. Again.

What was I thinking coming up here? Paul is seriously ill. I thought only about my own wishes, rather than what was best for him. How could I have been so selfish?

We flew home that evening and I notice a slight swelling in Paul's face. By the next morning, the swelling in his face was more pronounced and had extended down into his neck. The day after that—Tuesday—his right arm was swollen. While Paul was at the hospital that morning for his radiation treatment, the swelling was so pronounced that the radiation tech called Dr. Gerstley in to look at Paul.

Dr. Gerstley frowned as he pressed gently on Paul's neck and arm. "I'd like to have you admitted so we can see what's going on here."

He arranged for Paul to have a test that would image his veins and arteries. The test revealed that the tumor was now pressing on the large blood vessel that returns blood from the head and right arm back to the heart and lungs (Superior Vena Cava). Not only this, but a blood clot had formed, blocking the flow of blood and causing the swelling. Paul was admitted to the hospital, and started on a blood thinner in hopes of dissolving the clot. Blood was drawn frequently to monitor the levels of blood thinner in order to determine the correct dosage.

Dr. Gilliard, still Paul's primary physician, wanted another opinion. A vascular specialist came in on the second day, took a five-second look at Paul and left. A nurse returned to Paul's room five minutes later, looked directly at me, and said the doctor asked to see me. The doctor didn't know who I was, but he must have assumed I was Paul's wife. He hardly looked up from the chart as he said with an indifferent expression, "He has several blood clots causing the swelling. The Heparin might prevent more clots from forming, but nothing can be done about the ones that are already there. The swelling will never go away."

He tilted his head and grinned arrogantly, as if to say *I'm so glad I could be the one to deliver this bad news.* Dumbfounded, I couldn't speak.

Then with a sneer, he added, "I hope his affairs are in order. These clots will never dissolve, you know. He's a dead man."

Even if disbelief hadn't stolen my words, he wouldn't have heard anything I would have said. As soon as he delivered his pronouncement, he got up brusquely and marched away.

Too stunned to react, or even breathe, I sat motionless. That this stranger could appear to find pleasure in such a grave situation was beyond my understanding. When at last I breathed, the air did not make me calm, but carried the rage that had formed in my midsection into my veins, to spread throughout my body. I should have had the good sense to calm down before I returned to Paul's room, but I didn't.

I stood and marched back to Paul's room. He could see instantly that something was terribly wrong. "What happened? You're pale and shaking."

The words spilled out. Once I got started, it was hard to stop. Both of us expressed our outrage over the doctor's callousness. We wanted to lash out at someone, but who?

As our rage dissipated, the impact of his report hit us. The more we talked, the more we questioned why this doctor's prediction was so much more pessimistic than Dr. Gerstley's. Finally, Paul said he needed to be quiet and think for a while. I took this opportunity to do what I should have done before returning to his room—I went for a walk. A courtyard with a fountain spilling into a fishpond looked inviting. The trickling water and the chirping of birds in a nearby tree soothed me. I sat and watched the fish swim in lazy arcs, allowing my mind to calm down. When I thought Paul had had enough time to sort out his thoughts and feelings, I walked back up to his floor.

Inching the door open, I asked, "Are you ready for company again?"

"Yes. And I've made a decision. Just because that one doctor said that doesn't mean it's true. Doctors make mistakes. I want to get another opinion."

He rang for the nurse.

"Yes, do you need something?" the nurse asked.

"Indeed I do. Please get me Dr. Gerstley *and* Dr. Gilliard on the phone."

"Sir, it's so late, I doubt either one is reachable by phone until tomorrow."

"Fine. Just leave both of them the message that I'd like to speak to them as soon as possible. It's important."

We were surprised when Dr. Gilliard, the pulmonary specialist, called Paul a half hour later. He listened to Paul's story, and then simply said he was sorry. He offered no alternatives, and implied that we should be resigned to the gloomy expectation of the vascular specialist.

"Well, that sounded like Dr. Gilliard doesn't want to be involved with me any more. I want to hear what Dr. Gerstley has to say."

We didn't hear from Dr. Gerstley that evening, but he called early the next morning. After Paul had repeated his tale, I watched as he listened to the reply. My heart rose up off the floor when I saw hope spread across his face.

Paul nodded slightly. "Really? Yes, I look forward to seeing you tomorrow morning." He hung up.

"He disagreed sharply with the vascular surgeon. His exact words were 'There's no medical basis for saying the clots never dissolve.' He said he's seen blood clots dissolve many times. He'll stop in to see me first thing in the morning to talk about my treatment."

Finally, hope returned.

CHAPTER SIXTEEN

The next morning, Dr. Gerstley came in and sat down. He looked at Paul and said, "So he got you pretty upset, did he?"

"Yes, he did. He told Bettie, 'He's a dead man.' "

"Well, there's no basis for him to say that the clots will kill you. I expect to get these clots dissolved. It's probably going to take several weeks—don't expect dramatic changes right away. After a few days, we'll get the Heparin dosage established, and then we can switch you to Coumadin, the oral form. Then you can go home."

Paul's face relaxed. I was sure that he felt relieved that the vascular surgeon's opinion had been overturned. As usual, Dr. Gerstley shook Paul's hand with the kind of firmness indicative of a bond between two men with a common goal.

In the coming days, Paul would need the hope from that conversation, because his arms became more abused than pincushions from all the blood draws. After many adjustments in the dosage, the right level was reached and he was released with a prescription for the oral medication.

Paul's radiation treatments had continued while he was hospitalized. During this time, the side effects of the radiation had sharpened. Just as Dr. Gerstley had explained in the beginning, the radiation beam directed toward the tumor would also pass through everything else in its path, which included his esophagus. This was essentially destroying those tissues, making it painful to eat. At the same time, the cancer itself was robbing him of his appetite. Getting calories into him had become a challenge.

Never before had I thought of myself as a doting, overly-nurturing type. Until he got sick, Paul had cooked for me far more often than I had cooked for him. But now it was my turn to be the one in the kitchen. I did everything I could to get nourishment into him. I made protein shakes, prepared foods rich in fat and calories, and offered small portions to him throughout the day. Because I wanted to focus all my energy on Paul and help him in his effort to fight the cancer, I felt taking time to run was selfish. Paul had other ideas.

"I'm resolute about continuing to work throughout the treatment and beyond." He clinched his fist to emphasize his determination. "It's important for me to feel useful. I not only want to live longer, but I want the best quality of life I can, and working is a big part of that."

I tilted my head and half smiled. "I want to support you in that—which is why I feel selfish if I spend time running."

"But don't you see how guilty I'd feel if I'm the reason you'd make such a sacrifice."

"You have no reason to feel guilty. You didn't ask for this."

His eyes pleaded with me to understand his point. "But your running is important to you. And I want you to stay balanced so you can be there when I need you. The time you spend running is time you set aside for yourself and I think you need that now more than ever."

I thought for a moment. *If I run, I'll feel guilty for leaving him. If I don't run, I'll feel guilty that I'm causing him to feel guilty. I'm not sure I can win here. Better to preserve his dignity.* "Well, maybe you're right."

"So you'll still do the 5K this weekend?" His eyebrows went up.

"Yes. Yes, I'll do it. For you."

Meanwhile, Paul had decided he'd like to go his mother's in North Carolina for Thanksgiving. His only brother would be there, too. He wasn't ready to admit that he might not survive the cancer, but I could tell he was thinking more about his family. This was the first time since I'd known him that he had even mentioned making an effort to see them. When his mother had visited us a couple of years earlier, he had acted as if her visit was equal parts pleasure and annoyance. Now, faced with his mortality, he spoke about them more often.

We drove up on Tuesday, and I could tell the trip tired him, though he made a valiant effort to not let his fatigue show, especially to his mother. He tried to explain to Mary that he could eat only soft foods, but she insisted on preparing the "normal" Thanksgiving turkey dinner. Maybe it was because she didn't know what else to prepare, or maybe she didn't want to accept Paul's condition—it must have been painful for her to accept that her son might be terminally ill. In spite of his explanations to her, she showed some impatience when he was unable to eat turkey, dressing, green beans, and apple pie. Before he had come to the table, he had used his throat spray designed to numb the esophagus so that eating was less painful. He managed some mashed potatoes, but couldn't even attempt turkey.

His brother Marty showed a little more understanding, and kept the conversation turned away from food in favor of discussing the Thanksgiving Day football games. For a time, they were just two brothers enjoying time together.

Soon after dinner, he asked me to make custard for him. This time, Mary watched carefully as Paul first used the throat spray, and then still winced each time he swallowed. He continued to take tiny bites of custard as he and Marty watched the first game of the day.

Only when his discomfort was so visible did his mother begin to understand. After Mary saw the grimaces, the creases in her face seemed to deepen. Her eyes revealed a greater comprehension of the seriousness of his condition.

Paul later told me that when he saw the pain in his mother's face, he felt a moment of guilt over causing her to worry. Nevertheless, he told me he was glad we had made the trip to spend time with his mother and brother.

While at his mother's, Paul encouraged me to do my scheduled long run, because he insisted that I do the inaugural Disney Marathon the first weekend in January. Having assumed the role of coach, he didn't want me to miss a long run. I overheard him telling his mother, "Bettie's going to run the Disney Marathon in January. She just did one last month. Her training run this weekend is twenty miles." I smiled to hear him bragging about my running.

We drove through several nearby neighborhoods on Friday, measuring distances until we had calculated a twenty-mile route. Before I went out early Saturday morning, I estimated what time I would return. As usual, I gave myself a little extra time in case I had problems and walked part of the distance. I was able to maintain a steady pace, though, and got back to the house earlier than planned. Paul greeted me with a big smile, as if he gathered strength from my run.

"How did it go, Bet? You're back early."

"It went well. I was able to keep up my walk/run intervals and didn't slow much in the last few miles."

Paul glanced at his mother as he said, "Mom, do you know how many people can run a marathon?"

She shook her head and said, "No."

"Less than one percent of the population, according to *Runner's World*. And she was forty-nine when she ran her first one." Paul swelled with pride as he said it.

Mary smiled and nodded politely. If she was lacking in enthusiasm, Paul didn't seem to notice.

~ ~ ~

Paul had his final radiation treatment the last week in November. Dr. Gerstley said because the effect of the radiation is residual, we wouldn't know the full effect for another couple of weeks, so he wanted to do another CAT scan at that time. Two weeks later, Paul had the scan in the morning, and later in the afternoon, we fidgeted in Dr. Gerstley's office waiting to hear the results.

Paul reached for my hand as Dr. Gerstley walked in. The doctor's eyes avoided ours as he hung films on the light box. He pointed to the dark mass as he said, "The tumor didn't respond as much as we had hoped. It didn't shrink enough to consider surgery."

"So what's the next move?" Paul asked. He squeezed my hand tighter as he tugged at his mustache with his other hand.

"There is one other option—an even more targeted radiation."

"What do you mean?" Paul asked.

Dr. Gerstley finally looked directly at Paul. "We can insert a small device through your trachea and into the bronchial tube, and radiate the tumor from the inside. Since the beam won't be going through any other organs, a higher level of radiation can be delivered."

Paul shuddered and made a face of disgust. "It sounds like that would make my esophagus even... more, uh, raw."

"No, it won't, because we can direct the beam to go only in the direction of the tumor."

His expression changed to a resigned look. "Well, then, let's go for it. Like I've told you before, doc, I'm not going down without a fight."

I heard the words, but they didn't have the same punch as three months earlier. His face didn't reflect the same determination I'd seen before, although I was impressed at his attempt to be positive. I wondered if he was mustering bravado on my account.

I was unable to feign an optimism to match his. I remained silent. The report was too dismal for my fear to be reduced. Part of me knew the odds had just gotten worse—much worse. I quickly forced my thoughts back to him. I didn't have the luxury of thinking about my own reaction.

Dr. Gerstley's head angled up slightly, indicating his agreement with Paul's willingness to move on with the new treatment. "All right, but before we do this, we need to get a better idea of what's going on, so I want to do another bronchoscopy. Wait here and I'll tell you when we can you get in."

After Dr. Gerstley left the room, I tried to read Paul's face. I thought he was trying to hide his fear just as hard as I was trying to mask mine. *Breathe deeply. Stop picking at my cuticles.*

Paul clutched my hand tighter. "Well, Bet, whatever it takes, I intend to keep battling this thing. I'm not ready to leave you."

"I know. I'll be right here with you." I squeezed his hand tighter.

Once more, I wanted to know just the right thing to say. More than that, I wished I knew the right thing to *do*. Should we look for other doctors with other treatment options? Was it too late to explore alternative treatments? I wanted to believe there was still hope, if not for a cure, at least hope of buying more time. I conjured up mantra-like optimistic sentiments. *You can be one of the twenty percent. The mind is powerful. Unexplainable, spontaneous remissions occur.* The sentences wouldn't stick, though. They kept sliding down and draining away. What stayed in the forefront of my consciousness was that the tumor remained large, it still pressed on the superior vena cava, and it still threatened to cause more clots. And none of this took into account the likelihood that the cancer had spread. No one had mentioned anything about the lymph nodes that were already affected.

I forced myself to snap back to the present moment when the door opened and Dr. Gerstley came back in.

"I can get you in for the bronchoscopy a week from Friday at eleven. Dr. Gilliard will actually do the procedure, but I want to be there to see the tissue myself before I set up the details of the radiation procedure. The first high density treatment will be a week or two after that."

The procedure went as scheduled, but it revealed more bad news. The tumor had actually grown since the first bronchoscopy.

For weeks, I had been torn between spending more time at work and spending more time with Paul. I wanted to monitor Paul's medications, and simply spend time with him. At the same time, because Paul's ability to perform at work had diminished, I had stepped up my effort to work even harder, as if I had to work for the two of us. Besides, the company gave both of us remarkable support. We were never questioned when we had to be away, and the company president even gave Paul thoughtful get-well gifts. I wanted to show my gratitude. Paul's being sick was no reason that our contract didn't have to be performed.

Through all of this, Paul made sure I got in my long runs in preparation for the Disney Marathon the first weekend in January. I had gotten through the distances, but with a noticeable lack of enthusiasm. Running helped get my mind off Paul for short fragments of time, but soon my thoughts returned to the desperation of his condition. The driving force to complete runs was not to further my training, but so that I could report success to Paul. Each time I ran, or indeed when I was away from him for any other reason, I felt an invisible tether between him and me, tugging and pulling me home.

At three o'clock in the morning on the day of the Disney Marathon, I tried to dress quietly. My heart clearly wasn't in the marathon. I was more concerned with making sure Paul would be all right that I was with running down my checklist.

I eased out of the house at three-thirty, so that I could be parked in the Epcot parking lot by four-thirty, as required. In usual Disney fashion, we were directed into parking spaces. With an hour and a half to go before the six o'clock start, I settled back and tried to relax and stay warm. But I couldn't relax.

I might as well join the parade of runners going to the start area.

I glanced in the mirror before I got out of the car and saw that I had no pink hat. I had forgotten my hat. I couldn't believe I managed to leave the house without it, but somehow I did. *Oh, no, how can I run without my hat?* I knew it wouldn't make a lot of difference in the beginning, before daylight, but after the sun was up, and after I started sweating more, I knew I'd miss my hat.

As soon as I began to see people I knew, I got questions. "Is that really you? I don't know you without your pink hat?" "Where's your pink hat?" "Can you actually run without your pink hat?"

A friend said he had a spare cap in his car, which he let me borrow. But it was black. I continued to get remarks throughout the course, which was the only thing that lightened my mood. Each time I was alone, though, my mind turned to Paul. The theme parks offered only momentary

104

distraction from my worry. I wanted to hurry, not because I cared about my finish time, but because I wanted to get back home quickly. I left within a few minutes after crossing the finish line.

When I got home, Paul seemed fine and was curious to know how the run had gone.

"Let me see your medal."

"It's nice. It has Mickey on it."

"How are your feet? Did the socks and the Bag Balm work?"

I had tried soft, thick socks, but still got blisters during every long run. I had recently bought a pair made of two, thinner layers, rather than the standard single, thick layer. The fabric was soft, and the packaging guaranteed no blisters. They lied.

"Not so much. I still got blisters."

"Maybe it's time for something radical. Other runners joke about duct tape, but remember that picture of Bob?" Then in a television announcer's voice, Paul said, "You, too, can have silver feet."

One of the photos from last year's marathon showed one man sitting on the curb, his shoes and socks removed, his feet completely wrapped in silver duct tape. In the photo, he grimaced as he started to unwrap the tape.

"Well, I guess I have nothing to lose by trying it." *I'm not nearly as concerned about the blisters as I am about you, you silly man.*

The first high-density radiation treatment was on Thursday following the Disney Marathon. It took all day and was unexpectedly painful for Paul. Lengthy preparation was required before the actual delivery of the radiation. The medical dosimetrist, a technician who specializes in measuring doses of radiation, first took x-rays, and then had us wait nearly an hour while he made calculations. Then more x-rays and more calculations. Then the dosimetrist prepared the delivery system for the first treatment. Finally it was time for Paul to actually receive the high-density radiation. It was mid-afternoon by the time we left.

Because we didn't expect it to take nearly so long, we didn't take Paul's medicine, or even anything to drink, so Paul missed a dose of pain meds. By the time we got home, he was in severe pain, and I could see that the day's ordeal had stolen some of Paul's will. He looked not only physically tired, but also mentally tired. On the back porch, his sad eyes looked far away, and his face sagged.

He stroked his mustache in silence for a time, and then he said, "I don't know if I can do this anymore, Bet. I've been fighting this thing every way I know how, and yet it's still there, still growing. I don't know if I can go through another day like today. I'm beginning to think it wouldn't do any good anyway."

What could I say? Deep down lay the realization that no treatment existed that would help, but I couldn't admit that, even to myself. If he couldn't get better, then he would … no, I couldn't say the word, nor even think it. And I certainly couldn't take away his hope. Not yet. I had to keep up the appearance of hope. I had to put aside my feelings and keep my focus only on his needs.

I took a deep breath and hoped the right words would come out. "Paul, I understand you're tired right now. Today was harder than you expected. But after you get rested, you'll feel better, and now that the calculations have been done, the next treatments won't be as hard. Are you sure you're ready to just give up?"

"I don't know the answer to that. But right now I feel as though the quality of my life isn't very good. I don't want to give up, but neither do I want to go through more days like today."

"Well, you don't have to make any decisions at this moment. Rest for now, and let's see if we can get some calories in you."

I was just about to go inside and make him a protein shake and custard, when he added, "It just isn't fair, you know." He paused and nodded slowly. "But even after today, I still believe that I'm in my right place, and that all this is happening for a reason."

One of the things we had agreed on when we were first getting to know each other is that on some spiritual level, everything happens for a reason, and that where we are at any given moment is where we've put ourselves with all our prior choices. In other words, wherever we are, we are in our right place.

I did get up, but to go to him, take his hand, and stroke his cheek. I pressed his head against me. "I'm having a hard time accepting that this is happening for a reason. I hate this. I want the magic bullet that will make it all go away."

"You might as well accept it. Neither of us can change it."

"But I want to change it."

106

In a flash, he seemed to snap back to his old self. I felt his head lift up, as he straightened his back. His voice even had more energy. "Now, I need to get my strength back so I can get back to work."

"Okay, you rest and I'll get you something to eat." A few minutes later I brought him a shake, but as usual he only got about half of it down.

CHAPTER SEVENTEEN

Because the high-density radiation treatments were to be a week apart, we were surprised to get a call from Dr. Gerstley the next day, Friday. He said he needed to do another CAT scan. Neither of us thought to question why. The appointment was set for the following Wednesday. Paul was feeling stronger that day and insisted on going alone. Ostensibly, he didn't want me missing more work, but I knew he also wanted to feel as if he retained a bit of independence.

He returned to work mid-afternoon, and was in a good mood— maybe too good. *Did the test go well, or was he covering up something?* "How did it go?"

"It was fine. You know how that goes. All I had to do was lie there, relax, and let the machine do its thing. I'm getting good at this." His smile included a tinge of smirk.

As an afterthought, he added, "The technician wanted to catheterize me, though."

"Why?"

"She said my bladder was full. But it couldn't have been because I used the bathroom just before I went in."

I was confused. "Well, did you let her catheterize you? Did anyone else say anything about this?"

"No." Then he added, "I've had enough of being poked and prodded. I just can't go through any more of that. Besides, can you imagine how humiliating it would be to have a woman do that?"

I understood he was tired of tests and procedures, and I understood it would have been embarrassing. *But why would the technician want to catheterize him if there was no reason? What could cause him to be mistaken about his bladder? Something doesn't add up.*

"Paul, this could be serious. If the technician was looking at your bladder, and saw it full, then something's going on. You need to talk to someone about this."

His upbeat look faded. His eyes looked away and he sighed, his energy apparently drained. "I'm not talking to anyone else today. If you're so concerned, you can talk to someone." But beneath his defiant bravado, I thought I detected a plea for help, for someone else to be responsible. Or perhaps he simply didn't want to acknowledge what he had already been told.

It was now late afternoon. I called Dr. Gerstley, who wouldn't explain anything to me on the phone, but said to have Paul in his office early the next morning.

By the time I told Paul about the appointment, he had become more calmer. His shoulders slumped a bit as he conceded, "Okay, I'll go, but only because I respect Dr. Gerstley so much."

So on the day that Paul would have had his second high-density radiation treatment, we were instead sitting in the doctor's office looking at the films from the day before. Dr. Gerstley pointed to one of the films and explained, "You'll notice that everything looks normal, except for this small, dark mass near your lower spine." He paused a moment, as if gathering strength. "I'm sorry to tell you that this is a new tumor pressing on the nerve that controls bladder function. The reason you didn't think your bladder was full is because your brain isn't getting the right messages."

"Could this also cause back pain?" Paul's deflated look reminded me of the afternoon after the first high-density radiation treatment, when he had wanted to give up.

"Sure it can. Has your back been hurting?" Dr. Gerstley's eyes seem to probe Paul's face for more clues.

"Yes, it has."

Recently, he had asked me several times to massage his back for him. *I thought it was just general fatigue and stress.*

"Why didn't you mention that before?"

"I don't know. I guess I didn't think it was related."

Dr. Gerstley sighed and pursed his lips. He seemed uncertain what to say next.

Paul broke the silence. "Okay, doc, give me the rest. I can see that there's more."

My heart nearly broke as I listened to Dr. Gerstley tell Paul that the remaining high-density radiation treatments had been cancelled. Paul had already received nearly the maximum radiation allowed. And now radiating the new tumor was more urgent, not only because of its effect on Paul's bladder control, but also because it was the cause of the back pain. Furthermore, as long as the new tumor pressed on that nerve, Paul would have to catheterize himself.

At the word "catheterize," Paul winced. But before he could protest, Dr. Gerstley asked Paul if he had seen a general oncologist.

"No, not since that 'chemo salesman.' "

"But I've been reminding you that you need a general oncologist. The cancer is spreading, and I can only handle the radiation treatment. I'm not an expert at pain management, or any other treatment you might need. I'm going to make an appointment for you right now."

If the word "catheterize" pushed Paul's buttons, the word "spreading" pushed mine.

"Well, I'm not going back to that last guy," Paul said.

"Don't worry. I know someone you'll like. His name is Castillo, and his office is nearby. He's a good guy. You'll like him."

After Dr. Gerstley put down the phone, he handed Paul a card with an appointment time on it: Monday at two-thirty.

A few minutes later in a nearby room, I watched a male nurse show Paul how to insert the catheter, while an embarrassed Paul fought back tears. He looked as broken as a ten-year-old boy who had just had his bicycle stolen, and with it, his freedom. His face reddened as the nurse showed him how to attach a collection bag. In a strange way, at least for the moment, the catheter process had distracted Paul from the more sobering news—the cancer had spread.

If I had held onto some small scrap of hope until then, the appearance of this new tumor yanked it away, marking the end of my belief that a miracle could happen. I now considered the aches in Paul's legs and other locations on his back. Could those be the sites of more tumors? I feared the answer was yes. I remained quiet while Paul and the nurse got everything in place and Paul got dressed to leave.

On the drive home, Paul seemed far away. I was quiet, too. Nothing I could say would make the situation any easier for him.

Finally, he turned toward me. "I feel like half a man. It's not enough that I'm weak, that I can't eat normally, and that I can't stay awake all day. Now, I can't even take a leak by myself."

That's not the worst part, though. I need to keep him from thinking about the fact that the cancer is spreading.

"Paul, those things don't make you a man."

"You don't understand. It's not happening to you."

"You're right. I'm sure I don't understand. So tell me what it's like."

"Well, you know how important it is for you to be able to run. Imagine if you not only couldn't run, but that you couldn't do your job either. Wouldn't that make you feel less of a person?"

I thought about those things that made me feel worthwhile. It would be devastating to have both those things taken away. "Well, maybe. It's true that I really don't know what it would be like. Which is why I don't know what to say to you. I want so badly to make you feel better. I want to make all this go away. It all seems like a cruel alternate reality. Once in a while, just for a moment, I expect to return to our former life, where everything is back to normal. I want us to awaken from this bad dream."

"Yeah, I know. But I don't think we're ever going back there. As hard as this is, I still believe that I'm in my right place. This situation is where I've put myself, somehow, and it's for a reason. I don't understand the reason, but I believe there is one."

While we were talking, I noticed a subtle shift in Paul's body language. The defeat and humiliation had given way to a more relaxed, comfortable posture. I could tell he had found his way back to a place of peace and resignation. I only wished I could find that place.

By now, I didn't even think about going for a run. Paul hadn't said it, but every time I left him, his face sent the message that he didn't want to be alone. For the first time since I'd known him, I saw something in his eyes that resembled fear.

The backaches grew more severe, and so Paul's pain medication was increased. This caused him to be even more drowsy and foggy while he was at work, but he said he still wanted to go in every day. He sort of knew he wasn't able to do much, but he said it made him feel useful to be there.

112

On Friday, January 14, we went to see the oncologist Dr. Gerstley had recommended—Dr. Raul Castillo. He was just as Dr. Gerstley had promised, greeting Paul with a warm handshake, and listening patiently as Paul described what he had been through. While Dr. Castillo asked questions and listened to answers, he assessed Paul's reflexes and the muscle strength in his arms and legs.

Dr. Castillo asked if he had pain anywhere other than his back, and he asked if Paul had bad headaches.

"No headaches. But one leg aches sometimes." Paul absentmindedly rubbed the back of his right leg.

"The reason I'm asking is because lung cancer likes to travel to the brain. I'm not seeing any indication of that with you, though. The other place it likes to travel is to the long bones, and I think that's why you're having the backaches, and the leg ache. It's probably invaded one or two ribs, and maybe a bone in your leg."

I wish I could say I was surprised at this news, but this is what I already suspected. Paul didn't seem to be surprised, either.

Dr. Castillo changed the pain medication to something more powerful. Then Paul, realizing he had found someone willing to answer his questions, asked, "Tell me, doc, did I make the right decision to forgo chemo?"

"I can't say for certain, but probably. Chemotherapy hasn't proven very effective with your cancer type—squamous cell carcinoma. The radiation treatment you had was much more promising."

Paul nodded slowly, as if he was comforted by that opinion. Then he asked, "Well, then, what are my chances now?"

Dr. Castillo hesitated briefly while he looked through Paul's file. He raised his eyes to meet Paul's. "I wish I could give you more hope, but you deserve to know the truth. You've been through too much already to be misled now. The statistics say that from the time you were diagnosed, you had less than an eighteen percent chance of survival." Dr. Castillo spoke in a compassionate tone without sounding patronizing. I could see why Dr. Gerstley had recommended him; rare is the person who can deal with dying patients with such a combination of tenderness and candor.

As I listened to this exchange, I gauged Paul's reaction. Would he still cling to any hope that he could survive? His next question answered mine.

"I understand that the cancer has now metastasized. So what will happen next? You need to know that I want to work as long as I possibly can. I'm more interested in the quality of my life than the quantity."

"Of course, I understand. Then I'm going give you medications that will keep you comfortable while allowing you to stay alert. Now I have to ask you a hard question. Have you put your affairs in order? Are there things concerning your family that you need to take care of?"

Uh-oh. This was the first explicit reference to *the end.* Unexpectedly, ice water shot through me as I waited for Paul's reaction. He seemed relatively unfazed.

"No, not yet. There won't be that much to do. But I will."

"Have you contacted Hospice? If you haven't, I urge you to do so right away. They'll be a big help to both of you." He looked over at me. "Since they're so much closer to the patients, they're actually better than I am at managing pain and keeping patients comfortable, as well as providing support to family members."

That too didn't seem to affect Paul. "I don't think we need help yet, but we'll contact them when it's time."

Ah. Now I knew why Paul wasn't disturbed by these questions or the implications. On some level, he seemed to know what the final outcome would be, but was denying that he was approaching the end stage so quickly. I didn't want to think it was coming so fast, either, but Dr. Castillo's questions had delivered that message to me loud and clear. I now had an important job to do. I needed to help Paul get his affairs in order. That put me back into control mode—no time allowed to process emotions, just time to do what needs to be done, hour by hour, day by day.

We left Dr. Castillo's office with a new understanding of the inevitable outcome for Paul, but with each of us imagining a different time line. In the car, Paul said, "Well, I knew this was going to kill me eventually, but I thought maybe I had a year left. Dr. Castillo made it sound as if I won't last that long ... more like six to eight months."

Oh, my. What do I say now? That's not what I heard. "Paul, I've seen what this has done to you in such a short time. I hadn't expected as long as a year, but maybe half that. I think Dr. Castillo was trying to tell us that it'll be quicker than that. He wants us to call Hospice, which makes me think he believes you're going to need help soon. Maybe we should call now."

114

"Oh, it's too soon to call now. I don't need Hospice now. I'm still able to go to work."

He seemed to have a valid point, or maybe I was all too willing to be persuaded. Did either of us really need Hospice yet? Looking back, I now see just how much I wanted to agree with him. In the course of four short months, I had restricted my focus to little more than the present moment, and had become increasingly unable to see the future. If I didn't allow myself to think about it, then I wouldn't have to admit what was certainly going to happen, much less plan for it.

If I had known more about Hospice care, I would have known just how helpful they could have been to us then. We would have learned about preparations that would have made the coming days easier. We would have been better informed about what was likely to happen. If only I had known how quickly things would change in the next few weeks ...

CHAPTER EIGHTEEN

The conversation in Dr. Castillo's office emboldened me to bring up topics with Paul that I had lacked the courage to do before. I asked him what things he wanted to do while there was still time. Was there anything he wanted to do with either of his daughters? Things he wanted to tell them? I suggested he think about making a video tape to leave for them.

He replied that he needed time to think about it. A couple of days went by with no action; he said he would get to it later. At first, his inaction frustrated me until I realized that taking action would have been a clear sign of defeat, a recognition that he was going to die soon. As long as the bad part was in "the future," it didn't seem so awful. It was entirely different to think of it as imminent.

A couple of days later I was surprised when he announced that he had made a few decisions. He wanted his older daughter, Jennifer, to have his car, and he wanted me to have the remainder of his few other possessions. The proceeds of his life insurance was to be split three ways among his daughters and me, with Kathleen's share put into a trust fund for her future. Even though he had not done the kinds of things I expected— spend time together, tell them family history, share his wisdom—he had, nevertheless, been thinking about practical disposition of his things.

He also said that even though he was no longer a practicing Catholic, he wanted a Catholic service for the sake of his family—especially his mother.

I felt strangely comforted to know his wishes. It's interesting how the mind can seem to operate separate from the emotions. My mind knew that Paul would die soon, even while my emotions couldn't even fathom such a thing. Here was this person, alive, sitting here and talking to me. It was inconceivable that he could just cease to exist. Concurrently with trying to grasp that reality, a different part of my mind was able to focus on the practical, necessary plans.

After Paul had undergone five of the ten scheduled radiation treatments for the new tumor on his spine, Dr. Gerstley ordered another MRI. A couple of days later, we went the Dr. Castillo's office to discuss the results. He didn't tell us the findings at first. Instead, he said, "Paul, I want you to think about a couple of things. First, if you should get worse, do you want to be hospitalized, or would you rather stay at home?"

This was an ominous question, but it didn't take Paul long to answer. "I've already had one bad experience in the hospital. I want to stay at home, if possible."

"Okay." He made a couple of notes, and then asked. "Do you want to be kept alive on life support, or by the use of any heroic measures?"

"That one's easy. No, when it's time to go, just let me go." Paul's answers were ready, as if he'd already give them consideration. Apparently, Paul had been processing far more than I realized.

"If you want to make certain your wishes are carried out, I strongly suggest you sign a Living Will[9], and attend to any other affairs you need to. I'm sure Bettie will look after you as much as possible, but you still need the documents signed. Have you contacted Hospice yet?"

"No, but I will when the time comes."

Dr. Castillo shook his head slowly, and looked disappointed at Paul's answers.

Looking back, it's apparent that the latest MRI must have shown new cancer sites. Dr. Castillo must have seen how fast the cancer was advancing. He was trying to get us to act without alarming us, but we were both too blind to see the situation clearly. Time had stretched out for us, so that a week seemed more like a month. If we had taken a step back, and considered all that had happened in four months, we would have seen the swift progression. But we were so consumed with every small change— focused on hours and days—that we were unable to see what had happened in weeks and months.

"And how is your pain? Are the meds keeping it under control?"

"The pain in my back has gotten worse this week. And now it goes from my right shoulder blade down to my kidney area."

---

[9] A Living Will is a document that specifies what a person's wishes are regarding medical action to be taken in the case the person is no longer able to make those decisions.

Dr. Castillo changed Paul's medications to a combination that he hoped would offer stronger pain relief but that would still allow Paul to be alert enough to drive and to work.

In truth, Paul didn't drive often, and was nearly ineffective at work. But going there for at least a few hours each day gave him the self-respect he so desperately needed. He had continued to lose weight, too, including muscle mass. He was noticeably thinner and weaker. One Friday night, he spilled coffee on the bedroom floor. It wasn't a bad spill and I was right there, so I offered to clean it up. "No," he snapped, "I can get it up by myself. I'm not a helpless invalid, you know."

He managed to get an old towel, wet it, and kneel down to the spill. Watching him try to keep himself steady and clean the carpet at the same time was distressing. When he tried to stand, he didn't have the strength. I had been trying not to interfere or hover, but I couldn't stand back any longer. I stepped in to help him to his feet.

"I guess I'm more helpless than I thought. Damn, I can't even clean up spilled coffee." He lay on the bed and put his arm over his eyes, in an attempt to hide the tears. "Look at me. I'm not a man anymore. I can't do a simple thing for myself. I surely can't do anything for you."

It was an excruciating moment for both of us. I sat by him, and took his hand. Then I leaned my head onto his chest, but there was little I could do or say that would make him feel better. I certainly couldn't deny the physical weakness. All I could do was to explain that in the ways that accounted the most, he was more of a man than he could know. It was another of those instances when we were forced to inch closer to the reality of the disease destroying his body.

A week later, on Sunday, February 13, Paul and I were in our usual places on the back
 porch. Paul reminded me, "You know not to expect anything from me for Valentine's Day, right?"

"Of course. Nor should you expect anything from me. We've agreed on this from the beginning." We had long since believed that Valentine's Day was a holiday manufactured by the card, candy, and flower companies. We didn't need a holiday to remind us to express our love for each other, so we often surprised each other with something unexpected.

Paul then gazed out into the backyard, and abruptly changed the subject by saying, "I want to remind you that I want to be cremated."

"I know. We've always agreed on that."

"And I've decided where I want my ashes scattered—on the lake at Center Harbor in New Hampshire."

Paul's family owned a small house on Squam Lake, not far from and a little smaller than Lake Winnipesaukee. Though their primary residence was on Long Island, they spent summers in Center Harbor. He had told me numerous stories about the times he went there. More than any other place he had known, that place represented peace and contentment to him.

Before I could respond to him, he had dozed off. After a minute or so, he opened his eyes again, though he still appeared groggy.

He continued as if there had been no interruption. "And even though I'm not a practicing Catholic, I'd like a Catholic service. It's what my mother will want."

Oh, he must have forgotten that he already told me this. I was trying to hide my reaction when he faded out again.

When his eyes opened again, I said, "Paul, do you realize you just dozed off for a few seconds?"

"Yeah, I've been doing that for a couple of days now. I think of it as 'fade-outs.' "

That was the first time I noticed how pronounced these episodes were. *I should have seen this sooner. I haven't been observant enough. I need to pay closer attention.*

After an hour of watching him fade in and out, I recognized that he was sometimes a little disoriented when he "returned."

"Do you think this is significant enough that we should tell your doctor?"

"I don't think so. I think it's just the effect of the pain meds."

He had another "fade-out." This one was longer, and left him even more disoriented.

When he finally realized where he was, he decided to go in and lie down. When he did, he was asleep so fast, it was as if he had passed out.

While he slept, I paced around the house, looking in on him every couple of "circuits." *Should I be alarmed? Does this warrant a phone call to the doctor?*

Paul woke up about two hours later, but wasn't lucid.

"Paul, have you taken your medications?"

His answer was garbled. It was now after dark, which amplified the panic I felt. Until that evening, we had been partners in fighting the disease,

120

partners in handling Paul's treatment, partners in managing his medications. I realized I was going to be flying solo from then on. Paul was no longer able to make decisions, no longer capable of taking his meds correctly. Fear crawled inside me and then emerged through every pore. *What am I supposed to do now?* I wandered through the house aimlessly, trying to figure out what I should do.

At some point, I desperately cried out in silent prayer. *Please God, show me what to do. I don't how to do this. I don't know enough. Please keep me from making a mistake. I need guidance now more than I've ever needed it.*

I was reminded of the only other time I had felt this combination of fear and helplessness. Right after my divorce, I was so afraid of the responsibility of raising two children by myself that in the evening after the girls were in bed, I used to sit in the dark living room and rock, while crying and praying. That phase passed before long, though, as I grew accustomed to my new role, and moved into the future.

This time I couldn't imagine becoming accustomed to this role, and I didn't want to move into the future. Not a future without Paul.

After some time—I don't remember how long—I decided to call Dr. Gerstley. Of course, I only got his answering service. But he called back later that evening and listened patiently while I described Paul's behavior. He said Paul's "fade-outs" didn't sound like an emergency, but nevertheless he would like to see Paul the next morning.

CHAPTER NINETEEN

When we arrived outside the radiation oncologist's office the next morning, Paul turned to me. "Do you think you could go in and get a wheelchair? I don't think I'm steady enough to walk in."

It took me a moment to recover from the shock of his request. I wasn't shocked that he thought the wheelchair would be easier. But that he was willing to be seen in a wheelchair, which I knew would be humiliating for Mr. Independent-Work-Until-the-End, signified just how weak he must have felt at that moment. I tried to act as if this was normal as I went in and asked for a chair.

As I wheeled Paul into the outer office, I saw Dr.Gerstley round the corner and start toward us. He had not seen Paul for a couple of weeks. He did a double-take when he looked at us. His eyes widened and his jaw dropped a tiny bit when he first looked at Paul, but after a split-second hesitation, he managed a quick recovery. I instinctively glanced over at Paul and suddenly saw him through Dr. Gerstley's eyes. Paul had changed drastically in the short time since Dr. Gerstley had seen him. His thin, drawn face was nearly ashen, and his rounded shoulders slumped forward. With his weakened voice, he greeted Dr.Gerstley. "Hi, Doc."

Dr. Gerstley's face snapped to a smile as he reached out to shake Paul's hand. "Morning, Paul. Let's go into room three."

In the exam room, Dr.Gerstley glanced at me briefly then back at Paul before he asked, in the most upbeat manner possible, "So what's going on?"

"I've been dozing off periodically when I don't intend to. I call it having fade-outs."

"That's probably the effect of the pain medication. Anything else?"

"Yeah, I've noticed several knots on my back."

123

I didn't realize he had been examining himself that much, but I knew that he had not asked for back massages as much lately. I wondered if the knots were painful.

"Let me take a look." Dr.Gerstley lifted Paul's shirt and looked at his back. As he felt several lumps, I saw his face darken. He was slow to speak. "These lumps are new tumors."

"Well, can we radiate them? They've been hurting a lot."

Dr. Gerstley hesitated. "Uh, no, I'm afraid we can't. You've already had a lot of radiation, just about the maximum allowed." He paused, looking reluctant to continue, but knowing he had to. "The only thing we can do for you now is manage your pain."

That message was one that a part of me knew I would hear eventually, but it came as a shock nonetheless. Dr. Gerstley, who had tried all along to be hopeful, who had tried to foster that hope in Paul and encourage him to put up a fight, who had seemed to believe in Paul's will to overcome, had just said there was no hope. Though I wanted a moment to absorb that declaration and deal with my own reaction, I knew I couldn't allow myself to dwell on it. I forced myself to stay in the moment and be strong for Paul. It was my duty to be his support.

Paul looked up and in a weak voice said, "Well, you know what I've always said. 'When I can no longer throw the forty-yard pass, it's time to take me out of the game, coach.'"

Dr. Gerstley's eyes grew moist as he reached for Paul's hand. His face sank as he said, "I wish I could do more. The only thing I can do for you now is to send you down to Dr. Castillo's office. He'll manage your care and make sure you're on the best pain meds. I'll call now and ask him to see you right away."

Paul thanked him and they said goodbye with a firm handshake, a handshake between two gentlemen who respected each other, a handshake that was a final farewell. Dr. Gerstley didn't follow us out of the room, but remained standing quietly until we were out of sight.

As we proceeded down the outside walkway to Dr. Castillo's office, hot tears streamed down my face, in spite of my effort to remain in control of my emotions. I tried to hide my face from Paul. I couldn't see his face, either. I reached in my pocket for a Kleenex while we waited for the elevator. But I'm sure I couldn't made the redness around my eyes go away.

We waited only a few, silent minutes before Dr. Castillo saw us. After some brief discussion about Paul's pain and lucidity, Dr. Castillo changed Paul's pain medication and then added another to counter a side-effect. Then he looked into Paul's eyes and asked for the third time, "Have you contacted Hospice yet?"

Paul said we had not.

Dr. Castillo reached for the phone as he said, "It's time."

After he arranged for a Hospice counselor to meet us at home that afternoon, he asked his other standard question. "Have you put your affairs in order?"

Again, Paul said he had not.

"I suggest you do whatever you need to do right away. The cancer is spreading quickly and we can't predict where it will travel next. I think I explained to you last time that this cancer likes to travel to the brain."

I realized that, as an oncologist, he doubtless delivered that message to patients on a regular basis, but his face told me that frequency had not made it any easier for him.

He asked Paul if he had any questions. I expected Paul to ask him for an opinion on how long he had. But no questions were asked.

Dr. Castillo told us that he routinely followed the Hospice recommendations for palliative treatment, explaining that the Hospice nurses and caretakers were so much closer to patients in the last stages of cancer that they knew better than he did what was needed.

Paul seemed deflated and small as he feebly shook the doctor's hand to leave. I quietly wheeled Paul out of his office and outside. We were still quiet as I wheeled Paul to the car, got him settled, and then returned the wheelchair. After I returned to the car, we sat in more silence for a few moments. I had no words. I had no idea how he must have felt. I couldn't imagine how I would be reacting if it were me. Only jumbled feelings and numbness. If I allowed myself to express anything at all, the anger, sadness, and fear would all come tumbling out. I couldn't allow that. I had to be strong for Paul. It also occurred to me that he might well have been trying to be strong for me.

After a few minutes of my trying to gather myself, Paul turned to me and took my hand. "Well, old girl, you'll have to keep a stiff upper lip." This sprang from his many hours of British mysteries and, therefore, his love of British speak. I understood perfectly that he knew not only that his time was limited, but also that his control was limited. It was all on me now.

All I could muster was a faint, "I know, Paul."

So we began the drive home slowly, and in more silence. About halfway through the twenty-minutes he put his hand over mine and said, in the strongest voice that day, "You know, even though I don't understand why this is happening to me, I still have to acknowledge that I'm in my right place. I don't like it one bit, but I still believe that it's happening for a reason, that I'm in my right place."

What faith, I thought. Even now, he can still hold fast to his beliefs. Inspired by his faith, I replied, "Well, if it's happening to you for a reason, then it must be happening to me for a reason, because it's most certainly happening to me, too. I'm not sure I'm quite as accepting as you are, though. I just can't see any reason for this. In fact, I hate this."

"I don't say that I know the reason, mind you. But I do believe it's happening as it must. I believe the time will come when I do understand."

"I hope you're right, because right now I'm having a hard time feeling that way."

From his chair on the back porch, Paul said, "I don't see why Dr. Castillo thinks I should be in such a hurry to take care of my affairs."

Oh, dear! He must not have heard what I did.

While I realized that there must be things he needed to do, I also thought I understood his reluctance. Doing something to prepare for the end meant recognizing that the end was imminent. Neither of us wanted to face that fact. However, I also didn't want to have regrets that anything important was left undone. I was responsible for getting him to attend to anything important.

"Well, Paul, why not take care of these things now? Then you'll be done with everything."

He thought for a moment, stroking his mustache. "Tell me, Bet. How long do you think I have?"

That wasn't the question I expected. I paused long enough to try to come up with an answer. Dr. Gerstley said that the new tumors were an indication of how fast the cancer was traveling. Dr. Castillo took the initiative of calling Hospice himself—which seemed to indicate a certain urgency. It seemed to me that they both believed he had little time left. But I didn't want to be so cruel as to take away whatever hope he had of living longer. I had long believed that a prognosis could greatly affect a person's attitude and will. I didn't want to risk being responsible for robbing Paul of even one day. At the same time, I couldn't outright lie to him.

"I'm not sure, Paul. Castillo was insistent about contacting Hospice, but it's hard to know what that means."

"Why don't we call both Gerstley and Castillo and ask them?"

"Sure, we can do that. I'll call tomorrow."

On Tuesday, February 15th, shortly after arriving at work, I called Dr. Castillo's office. Unable to focus on anything important, I found busy work to keep my mind occupied while I waited for a return call. Paul stayed home that day, because it was too painful to walk. Even though he had seemed more alert on Monday, the "fade-out" spells on Sunday caused me to worry about him all day.

Early in the afternoon, Dr. Castillo called back. "Yes? How can I help you?"

"When we were there yesterday, we didn't ask your opinion about how much time Paul has left."

"Yes, I was surprised neither of you asked me that question." He paused, and apparently was reviewing Paul's file, then began to mumble. Finally, in a quiet, halting voice, he said, "It's hard to predict, but in my opinion, Paul has no more than a month." Then he quickly added, "Of course, no one knows for sure."

It took all my strength to keep my voice from cracking as I thanked him for his honesty, but I couldn't stop the trembling in my hand as I put the phone down.

CHAPTER TWENTY

There it was. A month! Even in the face of all we had heard, I had expected Dr. Castillo to say three to six months, which seemed infinitely longer than one month. Three months away is still in that hazy time of "the future." One month is now. Then I latched onto "no more than a month," which meant the end could come even sooner. A cold wave of fear swept through me as I realized how rapidly things were happening.

It just can't happen so soon, can it? How should I care for him? How will I get along without him? Is there anything I can do to extend his life? Those questions and more flooded my brain, until there was no clear thought.

I went to the bathroom, sat, and allowed tears to pour out, hot and profuse, allowing myself to be afraid. After some time, the shock lessened slightly, and my thoughts jumped ahead to the task of telling Paul. He was surely expecting to hear longer, probably six months or more. But I knew I must tell him the truth. He had heard so much bad news already—and now he would hear more. But it had to be done. I just hoped he didn't call before I left work.

I struggled through the rest of the day on autopilot, staying with tasks I could perform with little mental effort since my mind and heart were elsewhere.

At home, I first asked Paul how he had gotten along during the day.

"I did all right."

"Did you take your medications on schedule?"

"Yes, I think I did."

"How is your pain level?"

"It's not bad."

I saw that the shake I had made that morning appeared untouched. I saw a small, half-eaten bowl of cereal in the sink.

Soon enough, though, it was Paul asking the questions. "Did you talk with Dr. Gerstley or Dr. Castillo today? How long do they think I have?"

I sat down near him, took a deep breath, and mentally asked God for strength. "Yes, I talked with Dr. Castillo. He was hesitant to make a prediction, but finally he said that from what he saw yesterday, he estimates you have about a month."

Paul's face went grayer, and his mouth dropped open, but no words came out. He gazed out into the backyard. After a few beats, he barely whispered, "A month? I knew it was getting bad, but I expected he'd say six months … or at least three or four. A month!" For the first time, his eyes showed fear. Once again, I couldn't fathom what it must be like to hear that you have only a month left on this earth. It must be a little like being told the firing squad is loading their rifles. What was his crime? What was mine?

"Dr. Castillo was quick to say that's just an estimate. No one knows for sure."

Aware that there was nothing more I could say to give him either hope or comfort, I remained quiet for the few minutes it took to change out of work clothes. Then I sat beside him again. I took his hand, hoping I could transmit some kind of positive energy. A glance at the clock reminded me of the Hospice visit arranged by Dr. Castillo. "Remember the nurse is going to be here in a little while. Let's get you dressed."

At seven thirty, he was dressed and sitting on the sofa in the living room when the nurse arrived. I joined Paul on the sofa, and the nurse took a chair nearby. She explained the various services provided by Hospice.

"We'll send a nurse out each day to check on you, and we'll send a male nurse's aide to bathe and shave you. Also, we'll send a counselor out as needed."

As she spoke, I watched Paul. He tried to be matter-of-fact, as if this was routine, but I could tell the conversation troubled him. He was fidgety, unusual for him. Under most circumstances, he would have smiled and made small jokes. Instead, his face was taut, and his eyes looked apprehensive.

The assessment nurse gathered detailed information, such as how long since he had been diagnosed, what treatment he had received, and the state of his current condition. When Paul told her he had received aggressive radiation therapy but had declined chemotherapy, she agreed with what we had already heard about chemotherapy—that it wasn't particularly effective against squamous cell carcinoma.

Since I was the round-the-clock caregiver, she asked me about the medications he was taking. She also wanted to know about Paul's family, particularly his daughters. Then came more difficult questions, as if these had all been easy.

"Do you want heroic measures to be taken? We need to know in advance. If you do, then we are required to call nine-one-one to try to resuscitate you. If you don't, well, we need to know that, too."

"No paramedics, no life support. When it's time, just let me go. I especially don't want to be taken to a hospital." Paul looked at me almost apologetically, although he knew I agreed with him.

"Then you need to sign a Living Will. Do you have one?"

"No, I haven't done that yet."

"I suggest you do that right away. I have a standard form here, if you want it. You just need to have it witnessed and notarized."

Paul's hand trembled slightly as he reached for the form.

"Are there any other documents you need to execute concerning your estate or your children?"

"Well, I don't exactly have an estate, just a few personal possessions, a car, and a life insurance policy."

"You should think about who you want to get those things. You'd be surprised what can happen if you don't have everything in order."

Then the discussion became even *more* difficult. The nurse gently explained how the cancer would likely progress, and she described changes we should be prepared for, based on her experience with other lung cancer patients. She said the counselor would go into more detail during her visits.

The nurse's final task was to evaluate our home for Paul's physical needs. She asked to see the room where Paul would stay. As we showed her our bedroom and its adjoining bathroom, she commented that there was ample room for a hospital bed. As she started to describe the benefits of a hospital bed, Paul interrupted her. His chest swelled a bit as he said, "I don't want a hospital bed. I want to be in the same bed with her," and he gestured with his thin, shaky arm toward me.

She smiled and shrugged, as if to say that while his choice might not be the smartest one, she understood the emotion behind it. "All right then. Well, we'll need an oxygen concentrator. You'll need oxygen soon, and that's easier than having bottled oxygen brought in." She saw the door that opened from the bedroom onto the porch, and said the porch would be a convenient place for the concentrator. Having it outside would minimize the noise from the machine.

By nine-thirty, the intake nurse had completed her assessment. We were reminded that we would hear from a visiting nurse, a nurse's aide, and a counselor all within the next couple of days.

By Thursday, Paul decided he was strong enough to go to work. "I want them to see that I'm trying, and I want to get my work organized for whoever takes over." He managed to stay for about three hours, but was just too weak and shaky to stay any longer. He was so tired from sitting at his desk for those few hours that I had to steady him with my arm around his waist as we walked to the car. As I expected, he hadn't done much while he was there. His office mate told me later that he had had a number of "fade-outs." But Paul felt proud that he had managed to go in and had given it his best effort.

It seemed as if the effort he expended returning to work had used up what little energy and alertness he had mustered. By Saturday, his weakness told me that Thursday had been his last day at work. But not even I knew that was also the last time he would leave the house under his own power.

That Sunday, February 20, was my granddaughter's first birthday. I so badly wanted to be in two places at once. I was fearful about leaving Paul, but I wanted to celebrate Katie's first birthday. Three grandsons had preceded her, so the first birthday of my only granddaughter tugged at my heart. Sunday morning Paul stayed lucid for a couple of hours, a relatively long time, and we discussed whether or not I should leave him.

"Bet, you should go to the party. I don't want you to give up everything else in your life just because of me. Remember, Katie will have only one first birthday. And, besides, what can happen in only a few hours?"

Exactly. That's what worried me. But I thought he would feel guilty if I missed her birthday because of him.

I prepared his medications and asked, "Are you sure you can remember to take your meds on time?"

"Yes, I'll be fine. Go and have fun."

Reluctantly, I went to the party. It was fun, although I couldn't take my mind off Paul. I left much sooner than I would have ordinarily—my heart just couldn't get into the party spirit.

When I returned home and checked on Paul, he was foggy and faded in and out as he tried to tell me about his mother calling. "I think my mother called, something about..." A few minutes later, "Were you here when my mother called? I don't think I made very good sense..." Then, "I should call my mother. I think she's confused."

After I made sure he was up-to-date on his medications, I called his mother. Mary said, "I'm so glad you called back. I couldn't make much sense out of what he was saying. He seemed to drift in and out. I had to shout at him to get him to respond. He tried to tell me about his condition, but he was incoherent."

"He calls those spells 'fade-outs' and I they're caused partly from the medication, but also from lack of oxygen."

"It sounds like he's a lot worse than the last time we talked."

"Yes, he is. The disease is moving quickly."

"I had so hoped that I'd hear good news, that somehow he would get better. But I can see that's not going to be. I'll come down to help when you need me."

Parents aren't supposed to take care of their dying children. And yet she seemed so strong. I breathed deeply, attempting to inhale some of her strength.

"I'll call again soon."

CHAPTER TWENTY-ONE

That night I realized Paul shouldn't be left alone again. Even though it seemed that he had taken his medications correctly, after seeing how disoriented he had become, I didn't trust that he could continue to do so. This meant that I couldn't go to work the next day, or the day after, or until ... I couldn't form words for after that. Also, I wanted to be at home on Monday because the Hospice nurse was scheduled for her first visit. The nurse assigned to us had been scheduled to come the week before, but had cancelled because she had been sick herself.

I remembered that it was only one week ago that we had seen Dr. Castillo. I never imagined that so much could change in just seven days. Now I was beginning to understand why his prognosis had been so bleak.

Monday turned out to be another of those "rally" days for Paul. He awoke early and was more alert than he had been the night before. He was able to shower and dress on his own, and was sitting up when the nurse arrived.

The nurse looked at him and then at the notes from the intake nurse. Her eyebrows involuntarily went up a little. I suspect that what she saw didn't match the description in the report she was reading. He had declined quite a bit in the last week. If she only knew that this was a remarkably strong day.

She, like the intake nurse, suggested a hospital bed, explaining that it would enable his weight to be shifted easier. She said it could be placed alongside our bed. But Paul had not changed his mind. He told her emphatically he wanted to stay in "our" bed.

"Okay, then. Tell me all the places you have pain," she said.

"The worst pain is in my back, just under my right shoulder blade, but I also have pain in the back of my right leg and in my feet sometimes."

"The pain in your back, legs, and feet is probably because the cancer has spread to your ribs and other bones. When lung cancer metastasizes, it often goes to the long bones."

While they were talking, she noticed he was making an effort to get enough air. She said he needed oxygen and that she would have an oxygen concentrator delivered that afternoon. The nurse's aide would begin his daily visits the next day, and a counselor would come by soon.

Later that afternoon, with oxygen being delivered to him from the newly-installed concentrator on the back porch, Paul was slumped in a half-sitting position in bed. "This cannula bothers me."

I tried to adjust it to make it less irritating. "How's that?"

"Thanks, that's better. And it does make my breathing easier."

When the aide came the next day, Paul had returned to a less coherent state, but not so much that he couldn't explain, as the aide prepared to bathe and shave him, just how important his mustache was. "I've had this mustache since I was a teenager, and I'm not about to lose it now. So be careful with it." He lifted his arm to gesture, but it was shaky.

He's lost even more strength. I need to get him to eat more.

Because of his lack of strength and the complexity of the oxygen line, the caregiver inserted a permanent catheter so that Paul wouldn't need to get himself to the bathroom. Paul tried to protest, "What kind of man can't even go to the bathroom by himself?" But then he faded out, allowing the caregiver to complete his task.

On Wednesday, February 23, I recognized time was running out and we needed to execute the necessary legal documents. We quickly got the documents together and waited for Paul to be lucid enough that we all agreed that he was aware of what he was signing. By then, my daughters were helping, along with my friend Judy. Fortunately, Judy's husband was a Notary Public, and he came over to witness and notarize Paul's signatures.

On Thursday, Paul had a private conversation with his eighteen-year-old daughter, Jennifer, and also with Kathleen, fifteen, even though he was unsure how much she understood. Because of her autism, it was difficult to gauge her comprehension. Paul also spoke by phone with his ex-wife. I could see he seemed relieved after each one of these conversations, as if he were making his peace with the people in his life. And I was relieved to hear that Paul's ex-wife said she would come that weekend to take Kathleen.

I phoned Paul's mother. "You asked me to let you know when it was time for you to come down. I think it's time."

"Oh, I'm a little surprised. I thought we'd have longer."

I've been telling you. Haven't you been listening?

"He's getting weaker every day, and he's unconscious more and more."

"All right. I'll be down on Sunday. My brother John, and Paul's brother Marty will come with me."

I was disappointed it would be so long before she arrived, but she said it would take that long for them to prepare for the trip and then drive down. I didn't think she understood how fast the disease was galloping, or how seldom he was awake.

I should have called her sooner. What else should I have already done?

For the past several months, I had been trying desperately to take one day at a time, but now I was down to taking one *hour* at a time. I kept asking myself, what's the most important thing to do *right now? This day? This hour?* The first visit from the Hospice counselor helped in that regard. She made several suggestions, such as making a list of those persons whom I wanted to notify upon his death—prioritized. She also left a list of things to expect over the next few days or weeks.

One thing she suggested—that had not occurred to me—was Last Rites. While Paul had not been a practicing Catholic in many years, he had also told me he wanted to do everything he could to comfort his family, especially his mother. I knew that it would undoubtedly make her feel better if he had received the sacrament. Besides, we needed to get in touch with a priest for a memorial service.

Judy called St. James Catholic Church and arranged for a priest to come to the house on Friday. After a brief conversation in which we explained Paul's condition, the priest performed the sacrament—he told us it's actually called the Annointing of the Sick. Then we talked about a memorial service.

As soon as the priest left, the surreal atmosphere struck me.

I look out the window and wonder why the rest of the world is going on as usual? How can that be? Surely, this is a bad dream, and we'll all awaken soon and go back to our normal lives. Nothing is the same as it was just a few months ago. My world has been broken into little pieces, never to be the same again. Every moment of every day is unlike any I've ever known before, so radically different that it should be as obvious to everyone around me as if I were glowing orange?

The Hospice counselor had made another suggestion. "Continue to talk to Paul, even when he appears to be unconscious. Even when he can't respond, we believe he can listen and perhaps even comprehend. At the very least, we believe that patients recognize the voices of loved ones, and are comforted by that recognition."

She paused a moment, then continued, "At some point, you should give him permission to give up the fight. Often patients hold on even when they are in pain or discomfort if they believe their loved ones want them to. Giving them permission to let go allows them to make the transition easier."

The list she left was titled "Signs of Approaching Death." Scanning down the list, I knew I had already seen some of the signs: increasing periods of loss of consciousness, occasional jerking of the body, repetitive motions, the need to see a clock. Paul had begun to tug at the oxygen tubing repeatedly, resulting in a pile of coiled tubing on the bed, and each time he became conscious, he nearly always wanted to know the time.

Will there be no end to the number of times I'll be forced to face a deeper level of fear? To feel an even more intense pain in my heart?

Please, God, let me know what to do and when. I have only one chance to get this right. Guide me through this hour by hour.

When I was alone with Paul, I cycled between falling apart and being strong. Periodically, I took his hand and let my tears flowed uncontrollably. The hurt inside was as if a cruel hand was reaching in and tearing out my heart by bits and pieces. My eyes ached and my chest was sore from the gut-wrenching crying. But then I'd pull myself together, stand up straight, and focus on what Paul needed. I repeated to myself, *I need to stay strong now—I can fall apart later.*

On Friday, after the Hospice nurse had dressed Paul's growing bedsores, she asked, "Is there any reason he could be holding on?"

"Yes," I told her, "his mother, brother, and uncle are due in on Sunday."

She said she could see signs that his bodily functions were slowing down, and that he probably didn't have much time left. Suddenly, I was alarmed that he wouldn't last long enough for his family to see him. *I wish I'd called sooner.*

Another worry began to grip me. Paul had said how important it was that he remain in the bed with me, but what if he died during the night and I woke to find him lifeless beside me? I just didn't think I could endure that. I didn't sleep more than a little at a time, waking frequently to make sure he was still breathing.

On Saturday, Paul's ex-wife arrived and took Kathleen. Both Kathleen and I were relieved by this. She was confused by her dad's condition and glad to escape the house. And I was glad she would be spared seeing him worsen even more.

By Sunday morning, I couldn't get Paul to swallow his medicine. I called Hospice and they phoned a prescription for liquid morphine to a nearby pharmacy. But when Judy went to pick it up for me, we discovered that only some pharmacies carried Roxanol. What started out as a quick errand turned into a two-hour mission. With persistence, Judy finally located the medicine.

When I sat on the side of the bed to get the drops in his mouth, he groaned in pain from the movement. Just as I suspected, it had been so long since he had swallowed a pain pill that the effect had worn off. I just hoped his body would absorb the liquid quickly. I hated that he might be in pain but unable to tell us.

Later that afternoon, Paul's mother arrived, along with his brother Marty and his uncle John. They were shocked at the how weak, small, and incoherent he was. Hearing words are one thing, but seeing how the cancer had ravaged his body was another. As I suspected, Mary had not fully appreciated the severity of his condition until she saw him. But his appearance told the story. She went off by herself for a while and then returned to our room. She had left the room a wounded mother, shocked to see her son's life slipping away. She returned braced, as if she had digested the situation and was now ready to face what she knew was coming.

She asked me to show her a few things in the kitchen, and then she set about preparing an evening meal. It was as though she had been through this before and knew just what was needed most, unlike me, who could only focus on Paul. As I heard her cooking, I realized it had been several days since I'd eaten a normal meal.

During dinner, Mary told us, "Paul's sister Kathleen is coming in tomorrow."

Ever since I'd known Paul, he had told me about his deep affection and respect for his older sister, for whom his younger daughter had been named. I prayed he would last long enough to realize that she'd come to say goodbye.

CHAPTER TWENTY-TWO

By Monday, it was difficult to tell for certain if he had any moments of consciousness, but he seemed to stir more when his sister Kathleen spoke to him. We even thought he tried to respond to her.

On Tuesday morning, when the aide was bathing Paul, he noticed Paul's heart rate was faster than it had been. He said quietly that the increased heart rhythm was often observed just before the end, as if the body was making a final attempt to rally. I noticed that Paul's feet were cold, another anomaly. Paul was the only person I've known whose feet were usually warmer than any other part of his body. He often stuck his feet out from under the covers to cool them. We had joked about it, and he had never minded when I put my cold feet on his warm ones.

The Hospice nurse came around one o'clock, and reported that his heart rate was *slower* than it had been recently. When I told her it had been faster just a couple of hours earlier, she gently said this fluctuation could mean that the end was only a matter of hours away.

After the nurse left, I felt the time had come to give Paul permission to go. He had made his peace with some that were important to him, and the rest were there. There was no reason for him to suffer any longer. I began talking to him.

"I love you, Paul. I wish I could keep you forever, but not like this. You've fought hard, but it's okay to let go now. You'll always be in my heart. I'll cherish the gifts you've given me—the gift of your love, your complete acceptance. I'll hold dear the memories of the wonderful times we've shared. But I know you don't want this life, in a diseased body. It's time to go."

I kept talking and crying and talking and squeezing his hand. After a while, I was drained, talked out. By around four, I sensed that Paul's breathing was somehow different. I couldn't say exactly how, but I began to pay more attention. I had kept the TV on and tuned to programs that Paul would have watched, but decided to turn it off around five.

The lowering rays of the sun cast a pastel glow throughout the room, and also a calmness. I realized everyone in the house was quiet. This was an exception to the normal chatter of the last few days, with so many people in a small house. Five others were present—Mary, Paul's brother Marty, his uncle John, his sister Kathleen, and my daughter Linda—and yet I heard nothing.

As if instructed by an unseen force, I ventured out of the room to find Mary sitting at the kitchen table working on a crossword puzzle. "Mary, you might want to come in now."

Without a word, she brought a chair and sat on Paul's right side and took his hand in hers. As though the message had been silently transmitted, each of the others drifted into the room. I half reclined on Paul's left side and took his left hand in mine. Linda knelt beside the bed and held my other hand. The others stood at the foot of the bed.

The sun cast a nearly purplish glow throughout the room now, creating an ethereal effect. Adding to the scene was an unnatural quiet outside. The only sounds were softly chirping birds. The sereneness made it seem as if the entire world had slowed down just for us, because all of creation knew a life was ending.

Each of us began telling Paul "Godspeed," "Peace be with you," "We love you," "We'll miss you," "You'll always be in our hearts," and "It's time to rest now." After each of us had exhausted our final words to him, we silently watched as his face took on a tranquility that we hadn't seen before, and his body seemed even more relaxed. His chest rose and fell, a little slower with each breath. Then after one slow breath, there was only stillness.

Everyone nodded and, just as silently as they had entered, they each left.

I've tried so many times to envision how I would feel at this moment, and thought I was prepared. I wasn't. Can anyone ever be prepared for such a thing?

I'd said a lot of things to him in the last few days, but the one thing I hadn't said was "goodbye." Believing his spirit could still hear me, I said, "Goodbye, Paul."

I felt that a part of my soul had been ripped from me, and yet I was still able to appreciate how peaceful, even beautiful, his death had been. Just like he wanted. Here at home, surrounded by loved ones.

I phoned Judy and Karen, and then Linda took over, working her way down the list. Soon people arrived from Hospice and then from the mortuary. I stood by feeling so helpless.

On the way out, the gurney was stopped in the living room, and I was allowed one final goodbye. I kissed Paul's forehead and, on the inside, yearned for him to open his eyes and smile at me. In my mind, the gurney was forcibly torn from me, while I clawed and screamed. In reality, I stood stoically as I watched his body disappear forever. I was left completely empty. He had been my focus night and day. Now I had no focus.

I leaned heavily on those around me to get through the evening— and the next few days.

I caught myself time after time thinking what I would tell Paul— how great his family was, how good a cook his mother was, the stories they told me about him as a child. Then it hit me anew that I *wouldn't* talk to him again. This cycle of knowing but not knowing would continue for weeks.

Since Paul's family was all there, we planned a memorial service on Friday. I don't remember much about the service except that I most sat silently while tears flowed uncontrollably. My heart hurt and even if I was making a spectacle of myself, it didn't matter—I was powerless to stop. There must have been more than one song during that service, but the only one I remember is "Amazing Grace." I tried to sing, but my voice was so cracked, I soon gave up. More than ten years would pass before I could hear that song and not cry.

I also remember what I wore. About four years earlier, my mother had gone through a health scare, and Paul and I decided that I should be prepared to attend her funeral. We bought me a conservative, black suit. The irony was that I had worn that suit to two other funerals, and now to Paul's, and my mother was still all right.

CHAPTER TWENTY-THREE

By Saturday afternoon, everyone had gone and I was alone for the first time. I had been unsure how long I would stay away from work, but the emptiness of the house made me want to escape. I decided the sooner I returned to work the better. I needed to be busy.

On Monday I struggled to get up and go to work, not sure what I would do while there. I took my inspiration from Paul, who so desperately wanted to work as much and as long as he could. I managed to get myself to the office, and endured all those first, hesitant greetings. Most people didn't know what to say to me. "Welcome back" didn't seem to be the right thing. But neither did I know what to say to them. There were more than a few awkward moments. Somehow, I made it through the day, even if I did several times excuse myself to go sit in the bathroom and cry. Each time I felt a surge of grief, I'd flee to the ladies' room until I could get myself under control. As the week progressed, I was able to get just a little more done and make fewer trips to the bathroom.

At home in the evenings, though, I was paralyzed. I could do little other than sit at the computer playing solitaire. I just wanted to numb the pain. I had to keep telling myself repeatedly that Paul was really gone. Some part of me still expected to somehow return to our former life, wake up from the nightmare. I thought of things I wanted to tell him, rehearsed conversations until I once again realize that there would be no more conversations.

I couldn't find the energy to prepare anything that resembled dinner. Some nights I ate hardly anything except the candies in the candy dish on the desk. I had never been much for sweets before, but now I couldn't seem to get my fill. Or maybe it was just within reach. Chocolate chip cookie dough ice cream was another staple of my new diet.

One reason I wasn't eating better was that I hadn't gone to the grocery store since before Paul's death. Trips to the store with Paul were always an adventure, partly because Paul was more into food than I was and partly because of his playful humor. We'd start at the deli counter, where he ordered the proper blend of meats and cheeses for "nice" sandwiches. ("Nice" was Paul's highest praise for a sandwich.) From there we proceeded to the breads and condiments. At least I had persuaded him to use whole-grain breads, along with more mustard and less mayonnaise.

Then just before the produce section, we reached the bulk foods section, where there were open containers of candies and nuts. He said that containers were open so that customers could take samples. As he made his arguments, he reminded me of an impish, yet charming, little boy.

Coffee cakes, sweet rolls, and donuts often "appeared" in our shopping cart when I wasn't looking. After feigning surprise, Paul explained that "that little lady over there" must have gotten confused and accidentally put something in our cart by mistake. Then he said it would be rude to return the item to the shelf, so we should do the honorable thing and keep the item.

Shopping with Paul had always been fun. I couldn't face the store without him.

On the Sunday afternoon two weeks after Paul's passing, Sophie, one of our dear running friends—the one who had recommended pulmonary specialists for Paul—came over to see how I was doing.

After the usual preliminary conversation was out of the way, she said, "I think we need to go for a run."

"I don't think I'm up to that." I hadn't running for nearly two months. I had lost my will do to anything much for myself.

"Yes, you are. You need to get out of the house and in motion again. I know it's too soon for you to come back to the Sunday morning runs, but you need to make a start. Paul would want you to."

Something inside me resisted at first; resuming a normal activity seemed in a strange way to be disrespectful. *Can I do something as mundane as taking a walk?* But as I kept thinking about what she said, I knew she was right about one thing. Paul would want me to.

"Okay. I just need to change my shoes."

Sophie's insight proved to be just what I needed, because as we jogged—I normally hate that word, but that's what we did—we remembered the good times with Paul, before he was sick. I had been so consumed with memories of his last few weeks that I had lost sight of the importance of holding on to all the good recollections. She also suggested I find a grief support group.

After our very slow run and after she left, I was aware of how blessed I was to have good friends surrounding me, something I'd lost sight of in my darkest moments. For the first time, I knew I needed to start back on the road to running—and to life. She was also right that Paul would want me to move forward. I remembered how he encouraged me to run sometimes when I didn't think I had time, or when I wasn't in the mood. I recalled his face at the finish line of races. I felt capable of only small steps, but I knew I must make a start.

About a week later, when I got the call that Paul's ashes were ready to be picked up, I knew I wanted my friend Judy to go with me. This was a trip I didn't want to face alone. Judy and I had been close friends for more than twenty years. We had shared many joys together and also had propped each other up through many difficult moments. This time, I trusted that Judy's company would give me strength—and it did. Having her by my side made it easier to reach out and accept the cube-shaped carton containing Paul's ashes. There had been no need to buy an urn because Paul wanted his ashes scattered right away—on the lake where he spent his summers as a child.

I signed a few forms and we went to the car. I sat the box on my lap and took a deep breath, not sure what I was feeling. After a silent moment, Judy asked, "What do you want to do now, Bet?"

I thought for a moment and answered, "Will you go with me to the grocery store? I haven't had the courage to go since Paul died. But I need food."

"Sure, we can do that. But you don't need to go without Paul. We'll just take him with us."

I looked at her blankly for a moment before it sank in. *Of course, we'll take Paul with us.* As I was beginning to comprehend, Judy reminded me, "Paul would want you to have fun again. He'd see the humor in this."

"You're right, of course."

"We'll let him ride in the cart with us. That way, we can talk to him while we shop, and you won't be going without him."

"Okay, I'm ready." One look at Judy and I started to laugh, then I stopped. It felt strange. I'd nearly forgotten what it felt like to laugh. Then I started laughing again, and it felt good. I knew Paul wouldn't want me to cry for the rest of my life. He'd be the first one making jokes. I realized that's why I now needed Judy with me—to help me see the humor in what would otherwise be a dismal task.

We drove to the store, took the box in with us, and sat it in the child seat. We told him we were back in the store and asked him what we should buy.

I pretended to answer him. "All right, I'll start at the deli."

We then proceeded to produce, and then on to the bulk food section, where I explained to Judy Paul's philosophy about the "samples."

I even bought a coffee cake for him. We played "race cart" down deserted aisles, and giggled as we made car sounds.

"Watch me take this corner, Paul. What's that? No, I can't go any faster."

Judy asked, "Paul, do you need coffee?"

I asked. "Which brand of paper towels did we decide liked?"

As we were checking out, now with a lighter heart, I managed to keep the tears away when the store manager came over and asked how Paul was doing. That marked the first time I told someone that Paul had passed away without breaking down. (I *didn't* tell the manager that I had Paul right there, that he was in the box I was taking out of the cart while we were speaking.) After Judy and I were outside, we burst into laughter at the absurdity of the scene.

It was funny how everyday activities either got me down or kept me going. It was several months before going to the grocery store didn't cause at least a little anxiety. And I had to establish new buying patterns, since my shopping list had changed quite a lot. No Paul and no Kathleen. I frequently started to reach for an item, only to realize I was getting it because it was one of their favorites, but not something that I actually wanted, such as hard rolls for one of Paul's "nice" sandwiches.

A month later, I had reached the point that I could get through the day, but I still wasn't doing much better in the evenings. One night, however, I remembered what the Hospice counselor had told me. One cannot go around grief, or bypass it, or ignore it. Grief is a process that, sooner or later, one must go *through*. At the time I heard that, I thought I was prepared to deal with the loss, so I didn't pay much attention. Now, I felt as though I were struggling to not drown in a sea of despair, so I decided I needed to face it head-on. And I remembered Sophie's advice about a grief

148

support group. I began to attend not only a Hospice bereavement group, but also a second one that met at a local hospital.

I didn't say much during the first few meetings of either group, but as I heard others tell their stories of loss, I developed a greater appreciation of Paul's final gift to me—his acceptance of his death. One woman described how her husband had fought death to the end, becoming belligerent, and making those around him miserable. Another told of the sudden, unexpected death of her husband. We had had time to prepare, and Paul had given me the gift of going with acceptance and peace.

I also realized that my evening paralysis wasn't unusual. Several people reported a similar reaction to the loss of a loved one. Others responded by becoming work-a-holics. The counselors told us there is no "typical" response, no "right" or "wrong" response, and no timetable for the stages of grief.

It wasn't until much later that I realized another benefit of attending the two groups was that it got me out of the house two evenings a week, interrupting the pattern of sitting at home in front of the computer, eating candy and ice cream.

And my time with the computer was put to better use. I began journaling, a recommendation by a counselor at one of the groups. I wrote about the events leading up to Paul's death, I wrote what I was feeling at the time, and I wrote letters to Paul. After I mentioned the journaling to several friends, they urged me to write the whole story of my relationship with Paul and about the ordeal of his illness.

CHAPTER TWENTY-FOUR

I was making an effort to get back into my former running routine—two short runs during the week and a long run on the weekend. During a Sunday morning run, I encountered my friend Barbara, who lived nearby. She asked if I had signed up for a local race a couple of weeks away.

"I hadn't thought about it. I haven't been running a lot lately."

"You should do it. It would be good for you to see everybody."

"But I'd be so slow."

"That doesn't matter. What matters is that you get moving."

Watching her depart, I realized that I *needed* to show up at that race. Even though I'd probably be slower than I'd ever been, I also knew that Paul would want me to get back to the local races. He'd want me to see our running friends, and he'd want me to make it to the finish line.

By now, I'd become accustomed to talking to him—aloud when I was alone, silently when not. The morning of the race, I kept up a stream of conversation with him throughout the drive to the race site, continuing silently as I lined up at the start. I heard his voice speaking to me during the run, and also while I chatted with people afterward. That day, I felt a strong connection to Paul's spirit, perhaps stronger than any time since his death. Running was still keeping us linked.

In May, my company won a new contract. The program manager thought he was doing me a favor by giving me the position of lead software engineer—he believed the distraction of a new job would help ease my grief. He could have been right, although I didn't think so at the time. New contracts always brought stress, and all I wanted to do was glide through the day on autopilot, and then go home and eat chocolate chip cookie dough ice cream while playing solitaire. I didn't feel capable of doing real work—having to think and be present.

Keeping my job was necessary, though, and I forced myself to concentrate as best I could. Nevertheless, on some days the pain in my heart forced me into the bathroom to sit and cry. In the afternoons, almost as soon as I got to my car, the relief from no longer having to maintain a stiff upper lip was so great that tears would flow.

When the marathon training program started up again in late May, I eagerly signed up. I needed the discipline and I needed my running friends. I decided to try to get into the New York City Marathon[10] in November. I had never visited "the city," and Paul had wanted to be the one to take me there. Even though he grew up on Long Island, he had spent a lot of time in Manhattan. Often, while watching TV, he'd comment on a scene or a location he was familiar with and say how he wanted to show me places that were meaningful to him. In addition to wanting to do one of the biggest marathons in the world, I wanted to go to a city that had been part of Paul's life.

Meanwhile, I wanted to honor his last request: spread his ashes on Lake Squam (near Lake Winnepausaukie) in Center Harbor, New Hampshire. I'd kept in touch with his mother and knew she usually went from her winter home in North Carolina to the cabin on the lake sometime in early June. My daughter Linda and my friend Judy offered to go on the journey with me. I certainly didn't think I could do it alone. We decided to fly into New York City—a first visit for all of us. From there we would drive up to New Hampshire. Linda and Judy thought if we treated this as a vacation, too, it would soften the emotion associated with the task.

They were right. We arrived in New York on a bright Monday morning in early June and immediately became the quintessential tourists. After quickly checking into our hotel, we walked outside and started west on 49th Street. "We're here. We're in the middle of it!" exclaimed Linda. Judy and I gawked at the tall buildings with their beautiful details. "It's just like we see on TV," said Judy.

We headed for Broadway and soon were staring at the Ed Sullivan Theatre, home to *The Late Show with David Letterman*. We spent the rest of

---

[10] Runners weren't (and still aren't) required to qualify for this marathon, but the number of entrants far exceeded the maximum number allowed, so it was a race in itself to get the application in and hope to be one of the lucky ones selected.

Monday and all day Tuesday taking in the sights, sounds, and smells of the city. The next day, we rented a car and headed for New Hampshire.

We had a great drive up, and easily found Mary Quinlan's cottage. It's on a finger of the lake, stretching like a wide, blue ribbon in both directions. She made us comfortable and fed us well. The next day, soon after breakfast, in a quiet moment, we all looked at each other, no one sure how to approach the subject of the ashes. After a couple of beats, Paul's mother, not one to hesitate, said, "Well, I guess we'd better get on with it."

"Yes, I think so," I added.

"I'll get the rowboat ready at the dock. You all can meet me there in a few minutes," Mary said.

I had no idea how this was going to go. I'd never been involved in scattering anyone's ashes. In the movies, someone always had something profound to say, but I didn't know anything profound. I suddenly wished I had given it more thought before we left home. I wished I had a ceremony prepared. *I hope something will come to me at the right time.*

I firmly carried the box with his ashes and we all trekked out to the boat. We took turns rowing slowly out onto the lake. We were uncommonly quiet for four women, except for perfunctory remarks about the scene and the weather.

"It sure is a beautiful day, isn't it?"

"Yes, we couldn't have picked a better day."

The forced small talk revealed our unease. None of us was quite sure how we would go about the task, least of all me. But from the viewpoint on the water, I understood even more fully why this place could be special to someone. It was peaceful, with a ragged shoreline boasting a sprinkling of houses both large and small. A few fishing boats dotted the little arm of the lake where we were, and the ducks and geese provided the soundtrack.

We got about a third of the way across the water when Mary asked, "Do you think this is a good spot? The water is pretty deep here."

We agreed it was fine, although I was nervous because no inspiration had struck. I looked around, partly because I wanted to remember the location, and partly because I hoped a plan would come down from the heavens. No such luck. All three of them looked at me, as if I knew what to do. But all I knew at that moment was that the box had to be opened. I'm sure they saw apprehension on my face. I saw the same uneasiness on

153

the faces of Judy and Linda, almost as if they were looking at a Jack-in-the-Box, waiting for something to spring up. *Will there be anything recognizable? Do teeth burn?*

I slowly opened the box. Inside the cardboard was a plastic liner. A quick peek revealed granules of varying sizes reminiscent of vermiculite, the rooting medium used by gardeners. Beige and gold and black particles ranged in size from fine powder to small pearls. After we had all seen the contents of the box, and relaxed a bit that there was nothing recognizable or disagreeable, we all paused. Now what?

Mary, once again the leader, said, "Maybe we could say the Our Father." Hardly giving us a chance to agree or disagree, she bowed her head as if she were ready to begin. *What is the Our Father?* I was raised Protestant and was not familiar with anything called the Our Father. But then she began with, "Our Father, Who art ..." *Oh, thank goodness. It's The Lord's Prayer.* Judy and Linda must have had a reaction similar to mine, because we all three chimed in with "in heaven, Hallowed by Thy Name..."

I poured as we recited the prayer, slowly, because I didn't want to just summarily dump him out. But the prayer ran out before the ashes, so we began to chime in with remarks such as, "Rest in peace, Paul." "We hope you're at rest now." "We'll remember you always." "Enjoy your lake." As I got to the last bits, we looked at each other and smiles broke, then the smiles turned to laughter. We all agreed that if Paul were with us, he'd surely be cracking jokes.

When the box was empty, we all sat in silence for a couple of minutes. I relaxed. It was done. The final act I could perform for Paul. Part of me thought I should be sad about the finality of it, but instead I felt peaceful. I'd done what he wanted.

Mary broke the silence by suggesting that we tour around the lake a bit. We took turns rowing until we saw dark clouds forming in the distance and decided to head back to Mary's.

Later in the afternoon, I returned to the small wooden pier and walked to the end. I looked out onto the lake, and thought of Paul's ashes there now, sensed his essence spread throughout the lake. At the same time, I felt his spirit alive within me. "You'll always be in my heart, Paul," I whispered.

CHAPTER TWENTY-FIVE

Having returned to my marathon training group, I began to look forward to each run not as something I forced myself to do, but as a respite from the other duties of life, and as a time to feel closer to Paul. During those runs I learned to spend a little more time recalling the good times we had shared, and a little less time dwelling on the ache in my heart. As I ran, memories of his encouragement from the chair on the back porch, of our running together, and of his participation in the training program all flooded my mind.

During the next few years, I immersed myself in work—and running. I managed to do a marathon most years, still thinking that one marathon a year was a reasonable goal. A few local runners—Jules and Elyse Baclar, Beth Collins, Paul Morgan, Jim Sullivan, Layne Reibel, and a few others—spoke of the 50 States Marathon Club, and talked about doing one in every state.

Paul Morgan even decided to do all the states in one year. That meant a marathon nearly every week. *How could anyone do that?* We had been told that it takes up to three weeks to recover from any run over twenty miles. In addition to the physical demands, how could anyone afford the travel? I had to save up for one or two trips a year. He must be crazy—and wealthy. *Well, I couldn't possibly think about doing anything like that.*

Then a few of those "crazy" runners—whose numbers had grown—invited me to join them on a trip to Louisville, Kentucky.

"Instead of the usual t-shirt, you get a jacket," they said excitedly.

Well, sure. Airfare to Louisville, hotel room, rental car, race entry—but I'll get a jacket What a deal!

The argument was strengthened, though, by explaining that this was the first marathon in Kentucky in several years. No one could be certain that there would be another any time soon. In telling me about the trip, they also educated me about the 50 States Marathon Club. I learned that it could be difficult to find a marathon in some states, and they wanted to do Kentucky when they had the chance. Most of the members were not as committed as Paul Morgan. Most planned to do only a few marathons a year, taking several years to complete all the states.

Although I still wasn't thinking of joining the 50 States Club, the trip was more fun than I expected. We visited the Louisville Slugger factory, and the run was partly along the Ohio River. I came home grateful my friends had persuaded me to go with them. Why else would I have gone to Louisville if not for the marathon? I bought a magnet and mug, and enjoyed recalling the trip each time I looked at either of them.

A few months later, Beth Collins and the gang invited me to go with them to St. George, Utah. The marathon was a point-to-point[11], mostly downhill, unlike most courses that start and end at the same place. I'd never been to Utah, either, and Beth suggested we could see nearby Zion National Park and the Grand Canyon. I'd wanted to see the Grand Canyon for years, so the decision to join the group on this trip was easy.

We flew into Las Vegas and drove over to St. George, which involved going over Hoover Dam. The only part of the southwest I'd seen before was driving across southern Arizona, which is mostly flat desert. Here, the colorful mountains showed off the past in the many-colored striations of earth that had shifted this way and that over time. Mesmerized isn't too strong a word to describe my reaction to the mountains of southwestern Utah. The day before the marathon, a visit to a local site displaying dinosaur footprints added to the enchantment of the area.

When did morning begin? We got up at 3:00 and were climbing on buses at 4:15. I consider that the middle of the night. As the drive went on and on, I kept thinking, "We're going to run all this way back?"

The race started at six-thirty, just as daylight was breaking, and we were treated to sunrise in the mountains. Hues altered every few minutes as the sun angle changed. After just a couple of miles, the increasing light

---

[11] Marathon courses fall into three major categories. A closed-loop course starts and ends at the same place and forms a big loop. An out-and-back is similar to a closed-loop course, except that it goes out approximately half-way and returns along the same route. A point-to-point starts in one location and ends in another. Either runners park near the finish and are bused to the start, or runners park near the start and are bused back after the finish.

made visible the ribbon of runners that stretched in front and behind as far as I could see.

Just as promised, the course was mostly downhill, with only a few uphills in the early miles. I soon realized that I hadn't done nearly enough hill training in flat Florida. The downhills, steep in places, were taking just as big a toll on my quads as were the uphills. Also, the temperature shot up during the last half. I worried I hadn't put on enough sunscreen, and I felt as if I couldn't get enough to drink. I took two cups of water at most water stops, and even though my stomach felt full, I still felt thirsty. My stomach was queasy for the last few miles, and each time I switched from walking to running, I got dizzy. Getting to the finish line was a struggle, but I finally made it.

A few minutes after I finished, I reached the tables with water and snacks. I started to reach for water out of habit, but realized I didn't feel thirsty or hungry. In fact, I felt pretty bad—hot and cold at the same time, with goose bumps on my arms. Ten minutes later, I was throwing up in the parking lot. One of the men in our group, Jim, went to his car, grabbed a bag of potato chips, handed them to me, and said, "Eat these. You need salt."

Within a few minutes, I felt better. I asked Jim, "Why did the potato chips help? Why did you say I needed salt?"

"You have hyponatremia."

"What's that?"

"It's a little-known condition that results when you lose salt faster than you replace it. Some people don't get enough sodium from just drinking Gatorade. You need to take electrolyte replacement capsules."

Jim went on to explain more about the causes and effects of hyponatremia. I realized I had suffered from it before, but hadn't known what it was. I had felt queasy after marathons a couple of times. After my last Jacksonville Marathon, I had gone to the medical tent after the race because I was chilled and sick to my stomach. I felt thirsty, but couldn't drink or eat. The day was chilly and windy, so the paramedics only treated me for hypothermia, and seemed puzzled at the nausea.

As I nibbled on the chips, I thought back on my last few marathons, and it all made sense. When I was able to finish a marathon in about four and a half hours, I did all right until the finish. Sometimes I felt queasy for a little while, but I thought it was just low blood sugar and fatigue. When my times got longer, I started to feel bad during the last couple of miles as well as right after the race. Just a couple of months earlier, while everyone else in the group was devouring their after-race meal, I had wanted only crackers with mustard. My body must have known that I needed the salt. Soon after the crackers, though, my appetite for normal food returned.

Within about a half hour after eating the potato chips Jim gave me, I felt normal again and enjoyed my favorite after-race meal: a large Swiss and mushroom hamburger. I knew Jim was right. I needed to find a way to get more salt when I ran.

The day after the marathon, the whole group of us went to Zion National Park, where I was introduced to Step Two in destroying one's quads. (Step One had been accomplished the day before—doing a marathon on a hilly course with too little hill training.)

We drove into the park, found a large parking area, and drank in our surroundings. We found ourselves looking up at sheer, near-vertical rock faces on each side of the road. The face on the left was much higher and steeper, and a sign informed us that we were looking at Angel's Landing. As we kept looking, we saw minute forms moving near the top. Further inspection revealed more tiny dots along the face of the monolithic wall. We realized they were climbers. Then we saw people standing on the plateau on top of Angel's Landing. Beth Collins, Paul Morgan, and I decided we wanted to get up there—we had to find the way.

We went to the Welcome Center and were directed to a hiking trail that would take us up to the plateau. We loaded up on water and set out on the three-hour hike up the steep, switch-back trail. When we finally reached the top, the view was spectacular. We rested on rocks that seemed to have been placed there just to provide rest for the weary, and chipmunks entertained us as we feasted our eyes on the view, which included the opposite rock face and the road below. The red, orange, and white bands took on different tones as the sun moved overhead. When our stomachs demanded more than water, we headed back down.

By the time we regrouped with those who had remained on the canyon floor, my legs ached. I hobbled off to eat, convinced I'd never again walk normally. The combination of the marathon and the hike had succeeded in shredding my quads. But the view was worth every second! Looking across to surrounding peaks and down into the valley created the illusion of omnipotence.

The next day, Beth and I headed northeast to Bryce Canyon, where we hiked more. In the early afternoon, we left Bryce Canyon and turned south toward the north rim of the Grand Canyon. Unfortunately, by the time we got there, heavy rains had moved in and obstructed the view. Even through the rain, though, I saw enough to make me want to return and see more.

By the end of that trip, I understood why someone might want to do a marathon in every state. Why else would I have gone to Louisville or St. George?

Over the next few weeks, I investigated the 50 States Marathon Club, and discovered that one must have completed ten states to be eligible to join. I counted how many I had—seven to date. I needed only three more states. I also discovered MarathonGuide.com, a website that posts a marathon calendar. While I was still considering whether to join the club, I saw Jerry Sullivan from New Orleans, whom I had met at a previous run. He said he planned to run a marathon in Taos, New Mexico, in June, and suggested I run it with him. I'd heard about Taos for years, but had never visited that area. Now the marathon would take me there. My decision about joining the club was made during that conversation. *I'm in. I'm going to do this.*

Since I already had a mug and a magnet from most of the states I'd done, I started to deliberately collect one from each state I ran in—along with the finisher's medals. Each collection would be visible evidence of my progress, the magnets on the refrigerator, the mugs on racks in my kitchen, and the medals on the wall in the family room.

Meanwhile, I had ordered the electrolyte replacement capsules Jim recommended and was confident that my problems were over. I read more about hyponatremia and learned its occurrence is correlated to the amount of time spent exercising. A drawback of being slow was that I had to keep going for a longer time. People who finish a marathon in under four hours will probably never be bothered by it, but those of us who take much longer to finish are at a high risk. *Now that I know more about this, and with the capsules, I'll be all right.*

But the next marathon didn't work out much better than St. George, even though I had bought electrolyte capsules.

The week before the Taos marathon, Jerry called to say something had come up at the last minute and he had to cancel the trip. *Should I go anyway?* I had not traveled alone to a marathon, and felt a little unsure about it, but on the other hand, I didn't want to miss out. Add to that my thriftiness and the fact that my airline ticket was nonrefundable. *I'm going.*

I flew into Albuquerque on Friday and drove north to Taos. The marathon was on Sunday, so I had Saturday to see the area. I drove around Taos Mountain on the road known as The Enchanted Circle—and it lived up to its name. The spectacular views in several charming ski resorts and Swiss chalets was a treat in itself. But it was a Vietnam War Memorial Chapel that made an even greater impact. A large panel directly behind the lectern contained a large cross. On either side of the panel were long, thin vertical rectangles composed of a series of horizontal glass strips in various colors. The sunlight passing through the colored glass strips cast a kaleidoscope of colors on the wall of the chapel, creating an ethereal atmosphere. For me, this was the most "enchanting" part of driving The Enchanted Circle.

In the evening I went to packet pickup and pasta dinner, where I met several members of the 50 States Marathon Club, including Dottie Duncan. They made me feel like a part of the group before I even joined.

Race morning arrived and I met all seventy-eight other runners at the convenience store on the north side of town. As the start time approached, the race director gathered us and asked, "Is everybody here?"

We all looked around, and then agreed that we thought everyone was there. He then said, "Come on up to the cattle guard here. This is the start line." He then removed his stopwatch, looked at it carefully, and simultaneously pressed his stopwatch and said, "Go."

We were off. The night before at the pasta dinner, Dottie and I had agreed that we would stay together, doing the walk-run method at five and one's[12], for as long as we were both comfortable. Because of our early walk breaks, we soon lagged behind everyone else. We just smiled, content that we would overtake some of the fast starters in the later miles.

Support on the course was great, especially for such a small field of runners. We had Gatorade at mile two, and again at mile four. It was then that I realized I hadn't taken an electrolyte capsule.

I sometimes took Advil while I ran. I used small plastic bags for both the Advil and electrolyte capsules. I reached in my pocket for the electrolyte capsule bag, only to discover that I had brought the Advil, but not the electrolyte capsules. *Oh, no! It's hot and sunny and I'm going to be in trouble. The best I can do is drink as much Gatorade as I can and hope to get enough sodium.*

---

[12] Five and one's (5x1's) refers to a run/walk interval of 5 minutes running and 1 minute walking.

More miles went by and, as expected, we had passed eight or more others. At the half-way point, I was still feeling all right, but decided to adjust my run intervals to four and one's. Soon Dottie said she was slowing down just a bit, too, and encouraged me to go ahead. I probably went a bit too fast for the next few miles. By the time I approached mile eighteen, I was dizzy, and noticed my hands were swollen.

I walked to the next aid station, where there was an ambulance and EMTs. I asked if they had salt tablets, or anything salty. They said they didn't stock salt tablets, and they couldn't find anything salty. A boy of about ten stood listening to this exchange, although I was hardly aware of him. From past experience, it seemed I had only two choices. I could try to run again, and risk becoming even sicker and maybe not finish the race, or I could walk until I felt better. I opted for the latter.

About a half mile down the road, I heard a breathless voice behind me, calling out, "Hey, lady. Will this help?" I turned around to see the boy who had been at the aid station. He was running to catch up with me, and he was holding a small saltshaker. That salt looked like pure gold to me. I held out my hand, and the boy shook salt into it. I thanked the boy, and licked some salt.

The boy ran back to where I'd seen him. As I walked and ate salt, I smiled as I conjured up a scenario. The boy probably heard me asking for salt. Apparently he lived nearby. He must have run home to get the salt. In my mind, I saw him dashing into his house, and his mother looking up in astonishment at his hurry. As he grabbed the saltshaker from the table, she likely asked him, "Why are you taking the saltshaker?"

He must have said something like, "No time. Tell you later," as he dashed back out the door and ran to catch up with me.

It was an amusing and touching scene, at least in my imagination. Between that reverie and the salt, I felt much better by the time I reached the mile twenty aid station, where I had more Gatorade. I felt good enough to run again. I was able to resume a regular run-walk interval until the end. As I was standing at the finish line, having received my finisher's medal, I heard a small voice, "Hey, lady." I turned to find the same boy. "Did that salt help?"

"Yes, it did." I was so surprised to see him there. He was standing by a man I took to be his father, from the resemblance.

"You were my angel today. Thank you," I said to the boy.

I don't know how much he liked being called an angel but he smiled broadly. The man swelled with pride as he tussled the boy's hair and patted him on the shoulder. That boy made two people very happy that day.

About that time, I saw Dottie standing over near the food tables. She had finished about five minutes ahead of me. We were still snacking and chatting when the awards ceremony started, and we were both please to learn that we had each placed in our respective age groups—third place for her, second place for me.

On my return trip home, I wondered what the next marathon story would be. I had a notebook with me, and spent most of the plane ride home writing about the events of the trip. In addition to collecting medals, mugs, and magnets, I now wanted to also capture the memories.

CHAPTER TWENTY-SIX

Back at home and preparing for the next marathon, I continued to experiment with how many electrolyte replacement capsules to take. Some days I seemed to get it right, while on others I miscalculated—sometimes badly. There didn't seem to be a consistent formula, because heat and humidity were factors, too. Remembering the warnings from other runners that taking too much would upset my stomach, I was cautious about how often to take them. Should I take one capsule every hour, or every two hours, or every half hour? I couldn't seem to grasp that it was better to take too much rather than not enough.

Meanwhile, blisters still kept my feet sore and ugly. The inside of both my big toes and the first joint behind the big toes seemed to stay blistered. The nails of my third and fourth toes often dug into the neighboring toes. Also, my little toe turned under the fourth toe, causing the toe pad to blister.

I had tried thin socks, thick socks, double-layer socks, Bag Balm, Runner's Lube, New Skin, and wearing nylon footies under my socks. The one thing I had forgotten about was duct tape. When we saw photos of runners with silver, duct-taped feet Paul and I had joked about runners from Mars. I had used it once for the Disney marathon, and it worked fairly well, but that had been when Paul was sick, so I didn't try it again right away. By the time I returned to running long distances, I had forgotten about duct tape. Now, I was so tired of blisters, I decided to give it another go.

I ran the Austin Motorola Marathon in Austin, Texas, in February 2002. I had tried duct tape on my last long training run, and it worked pretty well. On marathon morning, I wrapped duct tape around my toes, as I had done before, and went off to the start. The first few miles went by easily. I appreciated the three different times called out at each mile. One person called out the split time, which is normal. Another person called out the pace, and a third called out a projected finish time based on the current pace. *Impressive.*

Around mile nine, however, something was hurting my left foot. I hoped it was just a sock that had gotten twisted, so I stopped and wiggled my feet, trying to rearrange my sock. But when I started to run again, the pain increased. It wasn't a familiar kind of pain. Finally, I sat on the side of the road and removed my shoe. The duct tape had started to separate, and the threads were cutting into the side of my foot. I had no choice but to remove all the tape from both feet, but now my feet had adhesive residue, a cut, and no lubrication. I struggled through to the end, but my feet were so blistered and sore I hobbled for the next two days. At least the day had been cool and my hydration was managed well enough.

I still hadn't found the magic combination of capsules and nutrition, however. In October 2002, I got to mile twenty-two of the Grand Canyon Marathon—yes, I had returned to the Grand Canyon. I took a few capsules in the early miles, but I was running with another woman who kept cautioning me to not take too many. It was pleasantly cool, but the humidity was low and it was sunny. In those conditions, it's easy to lose a lot of moisture and not be aware of it. At about mile twenty, I felt sick, so I told my friend to go on ahead. I hoped that if I walked for a while, I'd feel better. But the more I walked, the worse I felt. I took more capsules, but I had apparently reached the point that my stomach had already shut down. Walking slowed and then turned into shaky trudging, and I threw up a couple of times before I finally spotted an aid station ahead. I must have looked as bad as I felt, because as soon as the two paramedics saw me approaching, they started toward me. Unfortunately, they had no remedy to offer me except Coke. They, like most others, seemed to think it was low blood sugar.

Of course, the Coke didn't help. It was just something else in my stomach that came back up a little while later. When I got back to my room, I found a salt packet, opened it, and licked the salt.

I had learned that a brief rest, even as short as twenty minutes, had a powerful recuperative effect, especially if my electrolytes were out of balance. It's remarkable how much better I felt afterward, as if my body had been "reset."

Not finishing the Grand Canyon Marathon plummeted my confidence to an all-time low. In spite of that, I went with Beth Collins to

Des Moines, Iowa, in October. I took capsules more frequently and I finished, but I felt bad the last few miles and set an all-time worst record: 5:46. My times for the last several marathons before were barely more than five hours, so the slow time was quite disappointing.

Even though I still hadn't conquered the blister problem, I quit worrying about that. The blisters no longer mattered if I couldn't complete an event.

For the next year, my experimentation with capsules and nutrition continued. In the late miles of many long training runs, I questioned whether I should try to do any more marathons. I'm not sure what I would have said to someone who asked me why I persisted. Something hard to identify wouldn't allow me to give up. Maybe it was just stubbornness, but I couldn't simply quit. My other running friends were adding state after state, marathon after marathon. I was determined to figure out a way to push past this challenge.

After much experimentation, and believing I had finally found the right combination to take me to the finish, I traveled to New Hampshire for the Clarence DeMar Marathon. I maintained a regular pace until I suddenly felt bad at mile sixteen. I slowed my pace, walked more, and took more capsules at the next water stop. By mile eighteen, I felt even worse. My legs felt heavy and I couldn't get enough air. Dizzy, nauseous, and with swollen hands, I hoped I could walk the rest of the course. However, it wasn't long before I was throwing up—and too shaky to continue.

This event didn't provide course monitors or paramedics. I wobbled over to the side of the road, threw up, and then spotted a big rock, where I sat with my head in my hands.

A runner soon came over. "Are you all right? Is there anything I can do for you?"

"I'm sick. I need help to get back to my car."

"I'll try to send someone when I get to the finish."

Some time later—I felt so bad I don't know how much time has passed—a car pulled over to me. Inside was a middle-aged couple and an older woman. The driver asked, "Are you the one who needs a ride to the finish?"

Grateful, I answered yes. Then I noticed how nice and clean their car was. "I can't get in your car. I'm too sweaty, dirty, and smelly."

"It'll be fine. Don't worry. We don't want you sitting out here any longer."

Reluctantly, I got in. The air conditioning made me feel better immediately, and the people were so nice. They surely demonstrated the true spirit of Christianity.

After I got back to the car, I ate some of the potato chips I had bought for after the race, and soon started feeling better.

I was profoundly disappointed by the New Hampshire race, because after a year of experimentation with the balance of electrolytes and fuel, I had been confident I had found the right combination.

Is my body telling me I should just give up? Why can't I get this right?

Each time I was tempted to give up, I remembered how Paul had encouraged me, even when I had lost faith. *Paul wouldn't want me to give up. He'd want me to find a way.*

While out on a Sunday morning run, I encountered Jim, the runner who had given me the potato chips and explained hyponatremia to me. I described my recent experiences, and he said, "Take more capsules. In hot weather, I take one every couple of miles and it's not too much." I had been taking one every four miles.

About that time, I also discussed my problem with a nurse who seemed familiar with hyponatremia. She echoed Jim's advice. "After all, what can happen if you take too much? A little fluid retention? That can't hurt you. Hyponatremia can."

Why was I being so cautious? Probably because the warning of the other runners that if I took too much, it would upset my stomach. But I was getting the upset stomach anyway! In search of more information, I found several web sites that insisted hyponatremia is caused from drinking too much water, calling it "water sickness." But a couple of articles acknowledged that endurance athletes who release a lot of sodium and other electrolytes in their sweat need to replace electrolytes with far more than is found in sports drinks. I also learned that if the condition continues long enough it can cause brain damage—even death.

Deciding to take a more aggressive approach, I tried taking capsules at twice the rate that I had before. I also took one other bit of advice, which was to find a way to get more sodium delivered by the mouth. I started taking Frito's with me, but they have such a high fat content, my stomach didn't tolerate them well. Pretzels are saltier, but were too dry. After more tinkering, the combination that finally won out was Cheez-Its, Skittles, and energy gels.[13] The only drawback to taking Skittles was that my pocket rattled when I ran.

By this time, I had also gotten better at detecting symptoms early enough to make a correction. Humidity and temperature made it difficult to judge how often to take the capsules. If my hands started to swell, or if my stomach started to slosh or to feel full, it was time to take an extended walk break and get salt into my mouth.

By early 2005, I had completed several long runs and felt confident enough to join a group of local runners going to Fargo, North Dakota. The cool temperatures and my slow pace helped, and I finished feeling all right—not great, but good enough. My time was over six hours for the first time, but I didn't drop out. I made it to the finish line and I got the medal.

If I keep my pace slow and easy, and walk for an extended time when needed, I think I can do this.

This was state number sixteen—still a lot of states to go. But as long as I watched my salt intake, and aimed for slow times, maybe, just maybe, I could finish the states.

In September, having just turned sixty-one, I traveled to the Presque Isle Marathon in Erie, Pennsylvania. That marathon was also a 50 States reunion run. The club designates one run each quarter as a reunion run. A meeting is held the day before the marathon, during which club updates are given, awards are presented, and new members meet old members.

Of all the people I met that day, two of the more memorable were Norm Frank, whose marathon count was in the nine hundreds and who, at the time, held the record for the most marathons, and Lois Berkowitz, with whom I'd later share rooms and runs. I met people I'd read about in the club newsletter as well as new members, and members receiving an award for finishing all the states. The meeting was so much fun I decided to try to attend more reunion runs. Also, I met another member on the course the next day, with whom I would run many more times.

---

[13] An energy gel is a small packet of high-carbohydrate substance about the consistence of honey. Its purpose is to provide quick energy to athletes.

167

The course was a shady, flat loop around the island twice. At about half way, I found myself in the company of another woman about my age. "I'm Cathy. You were at the meeting yesterday, weren't you?"

"Yes, I was. I'm Bettie."

"What interval are you doing?"

"Four and one's. You're welcome to join me."

"I think I will. I've just been taking walk breaks when I felt like it, but I'd like to stay with you and your watch."

"Great. I'd like the company."

We ended up staying together the rest of the way. Even though I walked a lot in the last few miles, I finished in under six hours. I was surprised at how happy I was with a time of 5:46, since just two years earlier, I thought that time was dreadful.

More important, I now had seventeen states and more friends.

Still uncertain how frequently I should do marathons, I didn't enter another one until the following April, when I did Ocean City, Maryland. Because it was a point-to-point, runners parked in a large parking lot near the finish and rode buses to the start area. We gathered on the south end of the boardwalk and watched the ocean in the early dawn. The scenic course began on the boardwalk and proceeded north, the ocean on the right and quaint shops on the left. After a short distance, the course turned inland, over a bridge and through several neighborhoods where many residents came out to cheer and offer water and snacks to the runners. I approached the finish line feeling good—unusually good.

I had continued to experiment with how often to take electrolyte replacement capsules, and what to eat while running. Cheez-Its were still providing carbs and salt, and the Skittles provided sugar for energy. I don't know if it was just my day, or if my latest combination happened to be "the one," but I had the best run in several years: my time was 5:28—my fastest time since I'd begun having problems with hydration. My spirits soared.

CHAPTER TWENTY-SEVEN

Now that it appeared that I had found a method that would control my hydration, and with the realization that my body wasn't getting any younger, I decided to run as often as I could. It was somehow a relief that my only limitation was financial. Entry fees, airline tickets, hotels, and rental cars were all required expenses. I had no control over entry fees, and little control over airline tickets. I started contacting other runners about sharing rooms and cars by sending messages to the 50 States Marathon Club email group. Even with every effort to be thrifty, the average cost of each trip was several hundred dollars.

I chose Casper, Wyoming, in early June for my next race, just two months after Ocean City. At that time, I still thought a two-month interval was about right. I didn't have a travel partner for that trip, so I was free to set my own schedule. I'd wanted to visit Yellowstone National Park for year, and this was my chance. But first, I had to do the marathon. By this time, I had learned to run when the legs were fresh, and sight-see after. The walking helped to work out the lactic acid from the run.

At packet pickup, I was surprised to see Phil, who lived near me. I also met Holly, a wheelchair athlete and member of the 50 States Marathon Club. By now, I had become accustomed to seeing old friends and making new ones at nearly every marathon.

I thought Phil was quite a bit faster than I was, so I was surprised when I caught up to him at about mile eight. Phil was a marine, and looked every bit the part—short hair, wiry body, and willpower in his eyes. We leapfrogged for several miles, me going slowly past him when I was running, and he passing me when I walked.

The first time we were side by side, I said, "I know I'm not going fast, so it must be you going slower than normal. I expected you to be way up ahead. Anything wrong?"

"I've been having a problem with my knee recently, so I'm just taking it slow and easy today." And with that discouraging explanation, he left me again. We still stayed near each other until, at about mile sixteen, I started to feel my old symptoms again—swollen hands, shortness of breath, etc. I knew I had to slow down. "Take it in strong, Phil. I'm going to have to walk for a while."

The temperature had risen quickly, and higher than anticipated, and the last part of the course was in full sun. Still cautious about taking too many electrolyte capsules, I had once again allowed my sodium level to fall too low. I took two capsules and walked for the next three miles. I never got back to feeling good, although I managed to walk/run the last six miles. It was my slowest time ever—6:17—and I was third to last, but I finished. One more hard-won medal for my nineteenth state and thirtieth marathon.

After the run, I drove from Casper to Jackson Hole, where I spent the night. The next morning, I made my way through Grand Teton National Park and into Yellowstone. My first stop was the Visitor Center near Old Faithful. As it happened, the geyser was expected to erupt within twenty minutes. Because I'd read about Old Faithful since my early childhood, it was exhilarating to be right there, waiting to see it erupt in person. It was just as amazing as I expected.

An unexpected treat was the walking trail south of Old Faithful, peppered with many other geyers of varying sizes and colors. After that, a drive to several other locations in the park revealed more examples of nature's handiwork; it took the rest of the day, when it was time to leave for Denver and my return flight home.

Taking more electrolyte capsules seemed to have the effect of reducing my hunger during a run. I didn't think much about it, but I used only a few energy gels, and mostly nibbled on Cheez-Its and Skittles. Following Casper, I did Leading Ladies in Spearfish, South Dakota. My daughter Linda joined me on that trip, and handed me salt packets at miles sixteen and eighteen. Again, I managed to finish, but with slower times than I wanted and feeling weak and shaky. As usual, though, after taking in more fluids, eating salty foods, and resting for an hour or so, I felt fine. I finished in 6:09, only slightly faster than in Casper.

Beth Collins and Kay Ownby ran the New Jersey Marathon with me. We all started out slow and easy, which suited me fine. After a few miles, they were each eating an energy gel. Beth turned to me and asked, "Would you like an energy gel. You haven't had one yet, have you?"

"No, I'm not feeling hungry."

"But you need fuel."

"If I take enough capsules, I don't really need many gels or snacks."

"Well, don't wait too long to eat something."

I did take a couple of gels during the last eight miles, but I felt terrible after the run. The usual queasy stomach and lightheadedness.

After I was back at home, I mulled over Beth's question. *Maybe I do need to take in more nourishment during a long run.* I had been so focused on the electrolytes that I had lost sight of the need for nourishment.

On my next training run, I ate more, even though I didn't feel hungry. My energy level stayed more consistent and I didn't require as many electrolyte capsules. Even better, I felt all right afterward. Once I realized I needed more food, I considered how foolish I had been. Of course I should eat more. I had learned that years before, but had recently been so attentive to the electrolytes, I had lost sight of the importance of food during a run.

I remembered the time when I naively believed that if I just ran a handful of marathons, I'd have all the details worked out. Surely, it would be easy from then on. Yet here I was at my thirty-fifth marathon and still learning.

Feeling braver, I was ready to choose the next marathon. My friend LaRita Jacobs was interesting in going with me, depending on the destination and time of year. I looked for a marathon in the summer in a scenic location. Crater Lake Rim Runs, whose course goes around Crater Lake in Oregon, looked beautiful from the web site. A closer look revealed its altitude—5,980 to 7,850 feet—and its steep inclines. One running book rated the course as the third most difficult in the U.S. In addition to the degree of difficulty, the web site stated a six-hour cut-off. *Should I try it and risk dropping out again? But it looks so pretty and the trip would be such fun for LaRita and me.*

I emailed the race director, asking, "Should I sign up even though I don't think I can make the six-hour limit?"

He answered, "Runners don't actually have to finish the entire course in six hours. You just need to reach mile twenty in five hours. You can probably do that."

After stewing over it for about three weeks, I apprehensively sent in my registration and, more importantly, bought the plane tickets.

When I told one of my local running friends about my plans, he said, "I'm surprised you'd want to do that one."

"Why?"

"It's rated as one of the hardest courses in the U.S."

"Really? I didn't know it would be that difficult." *Uh-oh. Have I made a big mistake?*

I emailed the race director a second time, asking for reassurance that I wouldn't be left on the course, or worse, pulled from it. He answered back that he had been pulled from a race years earlier and had vowed to never leave a runner out on a course. He ended with, "Come on out and enjoy our marathon. I promise you'll be allowed to finish."

In August, LaRita and I flew to Sacramento, rented a car, and enjoyed the beautiful drive up to our hotel in Klamath Falls, Oregon. After we checked in, we headed up to Crater Lake for packet-pickup and for some sightseeing. The lake was even more beautiful than advertised, a unique geographic phenomenon—a volcanic crater that got plugged at the bottom, creating a lake with no water flowing in or out. The blue of the water is so brilliant it looks as if someone dyed it.

On race morning, I met several other 50-staters[14] and Marathon Maniacs (another marathon running club) at the start line. The description of the course by those who had run it before made it sound intimidating. No, not intimidating—impossible. But I was there at the start line, and I had the race director's promise that I would be allowed to finish. *It's time to see what I'm made of.*

The course, mostly on unpaved road, turned out to be a series of roller-coaster hills, so steep that I was unable to run going up and afraid to run going down. After only a mile or two, I knew I'd be walking most of the day. Occasionally, either across the top of a hill, or in a trough, I was able to run a short distance, but those patches were a tiny percentage of the course.

As the sun rose, so did the temperatures. The trail was dusty, the way my throat felt most of the time. I took plenty of electrolyte capsules, but they did nothing to make my legs stronger.

---

[14] Member of the 50 States Marathon Club call each other 50-staters.

However, the most critical factor was the altitude. The course started at about 7,600 feet, and rose to over 7,850 feet by mile fourteen. All that would have been enough, but the real test came at the end.

At about mile nineteen, when the course had become relatively flat, a police officer pulled alongside me and told me that the road was going to be opened to traffic soon, and that I should stay on the side of the road and watch for cars. I thanked him and moved to the side—where the footing was less stable. This made my progress even slower—just what I needed.

Soon I turned off the main road, though, and was again on a road closed to traffic. At the first water stop on this leg, a volunteer walked with me for a bit, asking me questions and looking at my eyes. I realized he was checking my condition to see if I was suffering from either heat exhaustion or altitude sickness. He must have been satisfied, because he backed off and returned to the water stop.

About that time, I became aware of a car trailing not far behind me. When I realized the car was the "sag wagon"—there to rescue a runner in distress—I knew I must be the last one on the course. The couple in the car maintained a respectful distance behind me—even when I made a necessary side trip into the woods.

The course passed by the finish area, which was *all the way down* to about six thousand feet in altitude—but still more than a mile high. It felt good to see people again, but I knew I wasn't finished. Here I learned I was not only the last one on the course but quite a bit behind the next-to-last runner. This made me uncomfortable for two reasons. First, of course, was pride. I'd been in the last few to finish before, but I'd never been dead last. Second, I had been raised to not be an "imposition" on anyone. I felt as if I was inconveniencing all the support people by being so slow, but I had no choice except to keep moving forward as best I could. I wasn't going to quit and not get Oregon in my quest for the states.

This was only a little past mile twenty-two, with roughly four more miles to go. The next two miles climbed four hundred seventy feet on a rocky trail before turning and coming back down. Already exhausted, I felt as though I were trudging straight up. And that's the word that echoed endlessly in my head while struggling up that part of the trail: trudging. Also, I learned that the sag wagon was no longer behind me. I guessed that the car's owner wasn't willing to drive up that steep gravel road.

Soon after I started up this climb, I met two men[15] coming down. I knew they were the next ones ahead of me. After that, I went so long without seeing or hearing anyone, I wasn't sure if I had gone out far enough or not. My mind started playing tricks on me. It surely seemed like I had gone two miles, but then I also knew that I should see some indication. What if I had missed the turn-around? Not thinking I had any energy to waste, I began calling out, "Hello. Anybody up there?" "Can anyone hear me?" I was so tired. My voice was weak—it probably didn't carry far.

I had to keep reminding myself that I couldn't do this much work and then not get credit for the marathon. I had to keep going until I had some reassurance that I had gone the required distance, even if that meant going too far. I forced my tired legs to move forward, although I could only go at a snail's pace. At last, I rounded a bend and saw an elderly man in a pickup, talking into a microphone connected to his HAM radio saying, "I see her coming now. She looks okay." Apparently, he had been waiting to spot me.

He offered me water, which I gratefully accepted, before I started back down the hill. Because the steep trail was sandy with small, sharp stones, I couldn't run downhill, either. My fear of falling and gashing my knees on those rocks was just too great. But at least I made faster progress going down.

When I got back to the finish line, I was astounded to see the clock still running. Two volunteers were waiting there to put the finisher's medal around my neck, and to give me water and food. The race director was still there, too. I shook his hand and expressed my gratitude for his patience; nearly twenty minutes had passed since the previous finisher. My time was 6:28, a new personal worst and my first DLF: Dead Last Finisher. Even with a time that slow, I felt such a sense of achievement! Only others who had run that course would understand what an ordeal it had been.

LaRita was at the finish, too, having occupied herself seeing more of the area while I was running.

"LaRita, I'm sorry I took so long. I underestimated how difficult this course would be."

---

[15] I hadn't met them yet, but those two men were Larry Macon and Frank Bartocci, whom I would later meet and see at many more events. Larry Macon has set the Guinness Record for the most marathons in a calendar year at least three times. As of this writing, he holds the record at 255 in one year.

"That's all right. I've been enjoying myself. I've taken several short walks and I've chatted with the volunteers."

"Thanks for being patient. Now I'm ready to get something to eat and get on the road."

After I ate, cleaned up, and changed clothes, we headed west toward the Oregon coast. We happened to see a drive-through zoo, Wildlife Safari. That stop turned out to be quite entertaining, as we slowly progressed through the "continents." Unlike most zoos, the animals were grouped according to their continent of origin, and their habitats were close replicas of their indigenous environments.

After the zoo, we continued on to the coast, and started south on the Pacific Coast Highway. I had driven a small section in central California, but this area was different. It seemed as if we were peering in on a movie set. From the way the road rose way above the rocky coast and then dipped down level with it, to the roiling fog creeping in, it was spectacular. We were in a trough an nearly sea level when we realized that the sun would set soon. We turned around and returned to a scenic overlook we had passed on the last crest, and got back just in time for sunset. We looked down on a fog layer that rolled in from the ocean, enveloping the coastline. I was reminded again how much more spectacular it is to see such a scene in person, rather than in film or photos. Pixels just can't fully capture the full impact.

After the sunset show was over, we headed south again and found ourselves driving into the fog that was rolling in—the same fog we had seen from above. The fog was so heavy that traffic came to a crawl for a short distance, but soon the fog thinned, and we were back to normal speed.

On our drive back to Sacramento the next day, we stopped in a small town for lunch. The locally owned café and its patrons seemed so typical of northern California, almost a caricature, that we decided we just had to see more of the small town. We happened upon a lighthouse that is picturesque enough to be featured on a calendar—the Trinidad Head Memorial Light—located in an inlet. A small park overlooked the inlet and the lighthouse and provided a great backdrop for our playful photos.

This trip was another of those made memorable not only by the marathon, but also by the sightseeing. If not for the marathon, I might never have seen that part of the country.

CHAPTER TWENTY-EIGHT

Completing a run as difficult as Crater Lake boosted my confidence to its highest level in a long time. I consulted MarathonGuide.com's[16] calendar and began planning races. I did Fox Cities, Wisconsin, in late September. I had a great time—5:33—quite an improvement over the 6:28 in Crater Lake. That was exhilarating! The big bonus was that I not only felt strong in the last miles, but also afterward, too. My car was nearly a mile away, and I was able to walk that distance without feeling too miserable. Sore feet, naturally, but overall not too bad. It helped that it was much cooler and flatter in Wisconsin than it had been at Crater Lake. Nevertheless, it was a delight to be able to run a better time *and* feel better after. Maybe my body had decided to cooperate.

Other runners had talked about the difficulty in scheduling a marathon in each state, but it was only after I had checked off quite a few states that I fully appreciated what they meant. At first, there were so many states to choose from that it was easy to find a state I needed in nearly every month. But now with nearly half the states checked off, I began to understand.

During some months, nearly all the marathons available were in states I already had. I conceded that I wouldn't always be able to do the event I really wanted in some states because of conflicts. For example, because I'd worked on a contract for Beechcraft in Wichita, Kansas, I'd wanted to run the Wichita Marathon. But that marathon is in October, a month abundant with marathons. A further complication is that some of the October marathons are the only ones for their states. Not having mastered the ability to be in two places at once, I concluded that I had two choices. I

---

[16] MarathonGuide.com is a popular site that maintains a calendar of marathons. It also collects results from nearly every marathon in the U.S. It is the "go-to" site for marathoners.

could stretch out my completion of the states, choosing two October marathons each year, or I could choose an alternative for some states. This scheduling business had gotten difficult.

I set up a spreadsheet of all the races I could find in states I still needed. I sorted according to date, and according to state. Using both of those lists, I marked a calendar with the location and date of each marathon in each of those states and made a tentative plan for completion.

For Michigan, I selected Grand Rapids, partly because it was on a good date and partly because it was a reunion run for the 50 States Marathon Club. I flew to Chicago and drove over to Grand Rapids on Friday, hoping to enjoy the drive. I didn't plan on a severe rainstorm that reduced visibility and increased drive time, causing me to reach Grand Rapids late at night. The next day was dry, though, and I was able to see a bit of the city before I went to the expo and the club meeting. The meeting was fun, and concluded with a pasta dinner to fuel us for the run the next morning. As usual, I renewed friendships and formed new ones. Throughout the run on Sunday, I chatted with other 50-Staters, making the miles go by easier. At the end, I was especially grateful that parking was so conveniently close to the finish, along with a large YMCA that offered us showers. That run marked the halfway point—my twenty-fifth state.

Jubilant for having reached the midpoint, and happy to have had some good runs, I decided the time had come to get this task completed. Who knew what the future held? I could become unable to run long, or at all, for any number of reasons. Many around my age had encountered various health problems. I already knew that each marathon took a greater toll on my body now at sixty-three than it had ten years ago. I still talked to Paul when I ran alone, still felt his spirit in my heart, and still heard his voice asking how it went, or telling me he was proud of my effort. But now I had other compelling reasons to run—a growing number of friends with whom to make plans, travel, and share running experiences. The friendships had become a significant part of my social life, and gave me added incentive and encouragement.

More eager to finish the remaining states, I went back to the spreadsheet, and moved races around to accelerate the schedule.

Among marathoners, and 50-Staters in particular, there are two phrases that have distinct meanings. "Back-to-back" means running two weekends in succession. A "double" means running two marathons in one weekend. I wasn't crazy enough to consider a double, but thought that an accelerated scheduled would require a few back-to-backs. The calendar told me that if I was serious about completing the states in the next two or three years, I'd almost certainly need to run on successive weeks, something I once thought was only for the radical marathoner. Could I do that? There was only one way to find out.

As a trial, I ran a long training run and two marathons on three successive weekends: a twenty-three-mile training run the first week; the Space Coast Marathon in Cocoa, Florida, the second week; and then the St. Jude Marathon in Memphis, Tennessee the third week. I ran faster than expected at Space Coast (5:42), but more surprising was that my time was even faster at St. Jude (5:31). The St. Jude finish was noteworthy for two reasons. First, I had learned that apparently back-to-backs didn't hurt and might actually help. Second, at twenty-six marathons, I was officially *more* than halfway.

Having made a transition in my thinking and planning, I had gone from occasional marathoner to a regular on the circuit. However, more lessons still lurked, waiting to be discovered.

Further emboldened by having run three weeks in a row, I began to toy with the idea of making it to the one-hundred-marathon milestone. That seemed like such a nice, round number, and it would make me eligible for membership in the 100 Marathon Club. My total was a mere thirty-seven, a long way from one hundred. For eight years, I had not repeated a state, thinking I wanted to make sure every marathon got me closer to the goal of finishing the states. I reversed that decision and set out to repeat states as often as possible to add to the count. An added benefit of doing races more frequently was that it kept me trained, since running more often appeared to be a benefit.

Taking advantage of Florida marathons, and those close enough to drive to, I repeated the Jacksonville Marathon and First Light Marathon (Mobile, Alabama). I finally ran the Ocala (Florida) Marathon, after hearing it recommended by other runners for years. The rural course by horse farms was as scenic and well-supported as promised. There, I broke 5:30 for the second time in two months. *Maybe running more often is good for me.*

After two more Florida marathons, I went to Phoenix for the Lost Dutchman. During that run, my circle of 50-Stater friends widened again when I met Amy Murphy. The hot sun was sapping my strength too much for me to run for long at a time, but Amy convinced me that if I walked fast, like I was speed walking, I wouldn't lose much time, and would conserve energy for the end. We stayed together until close to the finish, when she surged ahead. I finished only a few minutes after her, and felt better because of the walking. Amy was right about the influence on my time, but I also realized that it would have been all right if my time had been affected. Who else was paying attention to my times? My finish time meant nothing to anyone else. I didn't even remember my own finish times of past races, let alone anyone else's. The only important thing was to finish and get the medal.

I thought I had followed all the required pre-race preparations before the Lost Dutchman, but I apparently forgot one thing: I missed my ears with the sunscreen. The day had been sunny, and the tops of my ears were sunburned by the end of the run.

As a part of my new plan to check off states as quickly as possible, I had started doing what I had promised myself I would never do: plan quick in-and-out trips. Earlier, I thought I'd never make the effort to go to a new location without spending some time there, but if I were going to do marathons more often, I wouldn't be able to take extra time or spend an extra day in a hotel. So I began to fly in the day before a run, and then return home the afternoon after the run.

Therefore, I flew home from Phoenix just a few hours after finishing Lost Dutchman. Having checked out of my hotel early that morning, I had no place to shower. I learned from other runners that all I really needed was a restroom, and I could do a fairly good job of cleaning up and changing clothes. That afternoon, I found a Wendy's on the way to the airport. But late that night, back at home in my own shower, I winced as the warm water hit my tender, sunburned ears. I made a note to myself: don't forget to put sunscreen on the ears.

I not only learned to put sunscreen on the ears, but I also learned to put lip balm on my nose. My nose tends to drip most of the time, and especially when I run, and so I wipe it often during marathons. I often end up with a severely chafed nose and upper lip that peels just like a sunburn. One day as I was applying lip balm to my lips, I realized that it could also protect my nose. I never would have thought there would be so many things to remember for marathons. How much more would I learn?

From advice given years earlier, I knew to take everything necessary for the race in a carry-on. But I learned a few other things about marathon travel. After a couple of oversights, I knew I needed a way to make sure I didn't forget anything important. For example, on one trip, I had everything I needed for the race, but failed to bring anything to sleep in. My race t-shirt served the purpose, but I would have preferred a nightgown.

That was only a minor annoyance, but a few trips later I forgot my water bottle belt. Not only do I depend on my water bottle for my own fluid mix, but I also depend on the pocket in the belt to hold my energy gels. It was a good thing my shorts had pockets. I knew the heavy gels in the pockets would chafe my legs, but my greater concern was the lack of my energy drink laced with electrolytes. Fortunately, I made it all right, even though I did feel a little shaky toward the end.

After that trip, I decided to make a checklist so that I wouldn't let that happen again. That list has saved me many times since then. I developed a routine in which I collect everything I need on the bed, then use the checklist to make sure I haven't forgotten anything before I pack it all into my carry-on bag. Quite often, the list tells me I've overlooked something important.

Most distance runners have preferences regarding clothing, and I was no different. Nearly all pocketed shorts made for runners have the pockets along the back, just under the waistband. I don't like those for two reasons. First, if I have those pockets filled with gels, lip balm, hand sanitizer, Cheez-its, etc., I can't sit comfortably in the car on the way to the race site. Second, I need that space for my water bottle. I prefer shorts with roomy side pockets. I finally found a brand made for walkers that have that feature as well as one small pocket on the back. Perfect!

The lessons kept coming. I had met Jean Evansmore at Grand Rapids, Michigan. Via email, Jean and I arranged to share a room and a car in Oklahoma City for the Oklahoma City Memorial Marathon in April. Our room was in a motel that had clearly seen its best days long ago, but she and I made the best of it while we joked about checking for bedbugs. We agreed that neither of us needed much more than a bed and running water. After we picked up our packets and wandered through the expo on Saturday, we drove around the start area so we would know where to park the next morning.

On race morning, we left in ample time to reach downtown, find street parking that seemed close to the start, and join many other runners walking to the start area. A Methodist church, located a block from the start line, offered a hot breakfast to all the runners, along with shelter from the chilly temperatures, and, most importantly, indoor bathrooms. We gladly accepted the generosity, and a half hour later, we were off and running.

The temperature rose while we ran, but it remained windy. I had started with a lightweight jacket, and after a few miles, I tied it around my waist. By the last few miles, in warmer temperatures and a bright sun, it had gotten nearly as wet as the rest of my clothes.

I crossed the line first, and stood around the finish waiting for Jean. I put my jacket back on, but because it was so damp, it did little to ward off the chill. With every passing minute, the stiff wind cooled me more and more.

Even though it seemed longer, I'm sure it was only about twenty minutes later that I spotted Jean approaching the finish line. She didn't care to stay around the finish very long, and we soon started out to find the car. It was only then that I realized I hadn't paid attention to the street name or intersection where we parked. Tired and cold, with feet hurting, we trudged along, not sure if we were going in the right direction or not. Then we started laughing. We joked about how miserable we must have looked, cold and doing the "marathon shuffle."

We stopped a policeman, who tried to be helpful. "Do you remember anything about the street?"

"No, I wasn't paying attention, but I think it was northeast of the start area."

"I'm sorry that I can't help you. The only thing I could do is drive up and down each street. Unfortunately, I can't do that right now."

As he drove away, he shook his head as if he thought we were crazy.

We would have to do the searching for ourselves, and on our tender feet. Finally, after having changed directions at least three times, we spotted a familiar landmark and found our way back to the car. We laughed about it that day, but believe me, I've remembered to pay careful attention to where I've parked ever since.

CHAPTER TWENTY-NINE

When you start doing marathons more frequently, you might think you'd soon know all there is to know about running and traveling. Not so for me. Many marathons were fairly forgettable, but a few were memorable for one reason or another. Some stood out because of lessons learned, while other stood out because of the locations or interesting features.

Avenue of the Giants in northern California was unlike any other simply because the entire course is deep in the redwood forest—shady, flat, and extraordinarily beautiful. The Delaware Marathon course wasn't exciting because it consisted of repeated loops. It was made interesting, however, because the race officials put up a sign for every runner that had a distinction of any kind. My sign, a treasured keepsake, states that I was the oldest female runner.

For the Missoula, Montana, marathon, I flew into Spokane so that I could visit with my oldest grandson and his family in nearby Post Falls, Idaho. I hadn't seen them in over a year, so it was especially enjoyable to see my four-year-old great-granddaughter.

Because I wanted as much time with them as possible, I timed my departure for Missoula so that I would arrive about a half hour before packet pickup ended. Once in Missoula, I made a few wrong turns before I managed to find the park. I was shocked to find that nearly everything was broken down, and only a few people remained. When I asked if packet pickup wasn't supposed to end at six o'clock, I was reminded that it was now nearly seven. I failed to notice the sign telling me I was crossing from the Pacific Time Zone to the Mountain Time Zone. New lesson—pay attention to time zones.

The marathon was a point-to-point, starting in nearby Frenchtown and following a valley road back into town. It started at dawn, and the mountains, some still wearing winter white, were gorgeous during sunrise. The weather was perfect and the course runner-friendly. In the early miles, my pace matched that of Carol Goslin. Carol and I stayed together to the end, by which time we had become friends. Just in time for my Alaska trip the following month, Carol put me in touch with a friend who runs bed and breakfast just north of Anchorage.

Fall of 2008 brought a busy schedule. Only a year earlier, I thought it was brave to think of doing back-to-backs. That had now become normal. Because of my rush to check off states—and my limited budget—I decided to try a double (one on Saturday, another on Sunday), meaning two for one plane ticket. What's the worst thing that could happen? Not finishing the second one and having to return. Not such a big risk.

A popular double for 50-Staters is the New Hampshire Marathon in Bristol on Saturday, and the Portland (Maine) Marathon on Sunday. I arrived in New Hampshire on Friday night and found my lodging, which was in a barn—literally. A local horse farm had transformed a stable into a unique bed and breakfast. The stalls had been converted to sleeping spaces with curtains in place of doors. Unique, but not very soundproof.

The course was hilly, and I wanted to conserve energy for the next day, so I decided to walk up, run down. Surprisingly, in spite of a lot of walking, I finished in six hours on the nose. Apparently, the fast downhills made up for the slower uphills.

Another interesting feature of that run was that the finish was at a middle school that opened its gym and showers to the runners. I got a quick, albeit cool, shower before heading over to Portland, Maine. The earlier finishers had used nearly all the hot water—one of the drawbacks to being in the back of the pack.

In Portland, I took the early start offered to runners who needed more than six hours. Only a few miles in, we spotted Joan Benoit Samuelson[17] out for her Sunday morning run. Joan had remained one of my role models ever since I saw her amazing win at the first-ever Women's Olympic Marathon. My time was 6:46, my slowest time yet—even slower than Crater Lake. But it was still good enough for the medal. One weekend, two states checked off!

The only difference I noticed after the double was that recovery took longer than usual. It was Thursday before my legs lost the heaviness and fatigue of the two marathons.

---

[17] Joan Benoit was the winner of the first Olympic Women's Marathon in Los Angeles in 1984.

November brought the Marshall University Marathon in Huntington, West Virginia. The course enters the stadium, goes down the sideline to the far end of the field and then runs down the middle of the field to the finish line at the goal posts. Runners are given a football when entering the stadium so they can carry the ball into the end zone. I hadn't yet seen the film *We Were Marshall*, but it was still a thrill to finish by carrying a football to the end zone of Marshall's football field.

That run gave me a total of fifty-four marathons in thirty-seven states. Marathoning had become what I had wanted it to be all along—not *easy*, but possible. True, each run gave me sore feet, tired muscles, a few aches here, a few pains there. But nothing I didn't recover from in a day or two. Each one gave me a sense of triumph no less than the one before it. Crossing the finish line and having the medal hung around my neck has never gotten old.

Even though I didn't do any more out-of-state marathons the remainder of 2008, I did run another Florida marathon. It was in Clermont, a small town west of Orlando well-known to athletes for its hills.

I started out expecting my usual 5:30 to 6:00, but realized at the half-way point that I was on a faster pace than normal. I decided to push hard, and at the twenty-mile marker saw that my pace was good. I wondered if it was possible to break 5:30—not an achievement anyone else would notice, but one that would be meaningful to me. The last couple of miles were flat and the last quarter mile was a steep downhill; I stretched it out, taking advantage of that last downhill and charged as fast as I could to reach the finish line in 5:29! That was the first time I'd broken 5:30 since Ocean City, Maryland, more than two years earlier. Because it seemed that my times would inevitably get slower each year, I was ecstatic to break 5:30 again. I also placed first in my 60-64 age group.

In January, with thirteen states remaining, I flew to Nevada for the Running from an Angel Marathon, at a location between Las Vegas and the Hoover Dam that provided a beautiful view of the southwestern United States. The temperatures were mild but seemed much colder because of the fierce wind. I stayed warm enough while I was running, but I got cold quickly after my 5:53 finish. I was very grateful for the hot chicken soup provided to the runners.

By now, I had joined the ranks of other 50-Staters who arrived the afternoon before the race, and left the day of the race. This meant that I rarely had an opportunity for a shower, so I had developed creative ways of cleaning up and changing clothes. I learned that if I could find a family restroom, I'd usually have enough space and privacy to do a fairly good wash-up and change into dry clothes. If the water as warm, that was a special treat. I had also learned to take baby wipes in case there was no access to running water. At least I could wipe off most of the sweat before putting on dry clothes.

CHAPTER THIRTY

In most marathons, like other running distances, age groups are usually in five-year increments. After I turned sixty, I placed more frequently simply because there are fewer runners in that age bracket. In 2009, I turned sixty-five, and found that I placed even more often. Sometimes it was because there were only three in my age group, but occasionally I placed when there were more. In addition to the finisher's medals, mugs, and magnets from each state, my collection of marathon age group awards was growing.

As I traveled to more states, the ties with my running family grew stronger. I was privileged to see my friend Beth Davenport run her 100th marathon at the Yakima River Canyon Run, and I shared Fiona Wright's 50th state in Burlington, Vermont.

The sightseeing continued, too. In August, I did the Mesa Falls Marathon in Ashton, Idaho. Because Ashton is close to Yellowstone National Park, I stayed an extra day so that I could return to see more of the park. The geysers had not lost their fascination, and the alternate route back to Salt Lake City was a beautiful drive alongside mountains and lakes.

By November, I had only three states left, including Kansas. I marked that state off the list by visiting my friend Carol Goslin in Kansas City and running the Gobbler Grind in Overland Park, Kansas. During that weekend Carol and I made plans to go to Hawaii together. It was nice to know I'd have a good friend with me for such a long and exotic trip.

Scheduling the last few states was a challenge, and I would have loved for Hawaii to be last. However, I had to schedule it at a time that worked into my tutoring schedule because the Hawaii trip would be a long one. The choices ended up being The Big Island Marathon in Hilo in March for my forty-ninth state, and The Flying Pig in Cincinnati in May for my fiftieth.

Meanwhile, the Florida marathon season was underway. I ran Space Coast in Cocoa Beach, which had become one of my favorites. I saw many friends on the course, and I stayed surprisingly strong throughout, maintaining a consistent pace right to the end. My time was an astounding 5:16—the fastest time I had posted in more than seven years. *The old girl still has it. Woo-hoo!*

While I felt blissful about that time, I realized many marathoners would be horrified at being that slow. I've always expected to be in the last twenty percent of the field, and I've never been disappointed. Most of the time I'm unaware who the fast runners are at an event, much less their finish times. My experience, from the back of the pack, is decidedly different from those who run in the front or even those in the middle.

I've no doubt the three-hour marathoner can't imagine being on the course for four, five, or six hours. The lead runners have time to shower, change, eat, and return for the awards ceremony, all before I cross the finish line. But finish I do. Sometimes the food is nearly gone, or the finish line has been largely disassembled, but I get there eventually.

One of the reasons many 50-Staters feel such a strong bond is that for nearly all of us, our only concern is finishing. We're not competing for prize money, or even age group awards. If our time is slower than last year, so what? We prefer to enjoy the journey as much as the finish line. To quote several of my marathon friends, "We don't mind being on the course a long time. We want to get our money's worth."

Even though the 5:16 at Space Coast might not be impressive to many others, it was especially sweet to me because it was about a half-hour faster than I expected.

Two more sub-5:30s followed closely on the heels of the 5:16. It was thrilling enough to have one fast time, but to have three in a row was inexplicable. To what could I attribute my sudden improvement? I never found an explanation, but certainly enjoyed entering those times in my records.

After several more marathons in Florida, Georgia, and Alabama, it was time for the big trip to Hawaii. This was my first trip to the Aloha State, and I wasn't sure if I would ever go again. I wanted to take in the sights, so Carol and I planned to stay for nearly a week. Carol's granddaughter Hailey went with us as we flew first to Honolulu. While on the island of Oahu, we visited Pearl Harbor, the Dole Pineapple Factory, Diamond Head, and

Waikiki Beach. Then we flew over to Hilo on the Big Island, site of the marathon.

On both islands, I marveled at the open construction of many buildings, in which one outside wall is open. I first thought that since the weather is consistent year-round, open buildings made sense, but then I thought about unwelcome critters from the outside. If we tried that in Florida, we'd quickly be overrun with insects and lizards.

In Hilo, we had breakfast at McDonald's where the menu includes Spam and rice in addition to the regular items. We also saw the lava fields, the black sand beach, rain forests, waterfalls, and a macadamia nut farm.

Then it was time for the main event. We were bused to the start of the point-to-point course in the dark, and the sky was just getting light when the race started. The first half of the marathon course was scenic, much of it traveling along the coast and through rain forests. Because it was so early in the day, the first half also stayed moderately cool.

As the second half of the course wound inland, it didn't offer views as nice nor did it include shade. The temperatures soared and bright sun alternated with rain showers, causing my sunscreen to wash off. I tried to apply more, but it merely slipped around, refusing to stick in the sweat and rain. The last three miles returned us to the coast with its pretty views, but also full sun. I could feel the heat building in my exposed skin. I put my small race towel on my neck for much of the last two miles, in an attempt to protect vulnerable skin.

Hailey greeted us at the finish, where she had volunteered while we ran. I came in first, and Carol was only a few minutes later.

"Yay, Carol. We did it."

"Yeah, we did. It was hot out there."

"Yes, and I'm sunburned, but so glad to be finished. Forty-nine down. One more state to go."

"Let's see how we placed."

We walked over to the results table and learned that no one in our age group had finished before us, so I was first and Carol was second. We stayed long enough to receive our awards, and then it was time to dash to the airport and head home.

For my final state, I arrived in Cincinnati, Ohio, on Saturday and quickly made my way to the big expo and packet pickup for the Flying Pig Marathon. The expo was huge—one of the largest I've been to. It was so

189

crowded that at times I could only inch my way through the mass of humanity. In addition to my packet, I was able to get parking advice for the next morning: arrive an hour early and park in one of the public parking lots near the start/finish.

At what seemed like the middle of the night, I got up, went through the usual routine, including plenty of lubrication and sunscreen. I left for the race site in time to arrive in the area at five-fifteen for the six-thirty start. As soon as I was about five blocks from the parking area, traffic came to a crawl. The slow progress quickly deteriorated to stop and go, with more stop than go. I crept along for more than hour before I finally got into a parking lot at six-twenty. Race start was ten minutes away, but I tried not to panic, and reminded myself that even if I started late, there was no time limit. As I exited the car, I knew that regardless of the time, I required a port-a-potty before I could even think about running.

Luckily, as I started walking toward the start area, relying on the flow of runners for direction, I encountered a bank of portable restrooms. By the time I emerged, I heard a sound in the distance that I thought could be the start gun. I asked people around me if the race had started, and they said they thought so. The crowd was so large and loud, no one in the immediate area knew for sure what was going on. I joined the drifting mass of people, and about fourteen minutes later, reached the start line. Apparently, runners of several different distances were all blended for the extremely crowded start.

Incredibly, I did not see a single person I knew during the entire race. As I approached the finish line, I decided I'd have to make my own excitement. This was my last state and I wanted a celebration of my achievement. I raised my arms, waved my towel in the air, and yelled, "This is my fiftieth state!" That got a response from the spectators, who then cheered me in.

Still, it would have been more exciting to share my joy with someone I knew. It was a bittersweet finish. I was happy to have completed all fifty states, but as I sat in my car wiping off sweat with baby wipes, and putting on dry clothes, I was a little disappointed that there hadn't been any friends to celebrate with. I settled for talking to Paul, telling him I just finished my last state. I could nearly see his smile and hear him say, "Way to go, Bet."

CHAPTER THIRTY-ONE

On the journey home, my thoughts turned to future goals. I'd already committed to reaching the hundred-marathon milestone, but what after that? The answer came when I realized how many states I had done a second time. Clearly, a second round of the states would be my next challenge.

I still thought of Paul often when I ran, but there were other reasons to keep going. First, I couldn't imagine not having another marathon to look forward to. I had become connected to many running friends from across the nation. If I didn't continue traveling to marathons, I wouldn't see them. Nor would I have a compelling reason to get up early and run long on Sunday. Most of all, I'd miss that sense of accomplishment as each finisher's medal is hung around my neck. I realized I'd keep running as long as I could, regardless of how slow I might get.

After I announced my goal of completing a hundred marathons, several friends asked me why I continued to torture myself, especially when I described the various aches and pains, the trials of training, and the calluses and scars. Why wouldn't I just quit? By turns, my right knee hurts, my lower back hurts, both feet hurt from heel spurs, and I have a chronic pain in my right groin. Add to that the aggravation of the bone spurs in my neck. My toenails will never be normal; they all have fungus and are permanently disfigured. I have scars on my midsection from my running bra. I have unattractive tan lines from the edge of my shorts to the top of my socks. This is all in addition to the overall muscle soreness and deep fatigue that follows most marathons.

Even *I* sometimes question my own judgment in the last few miles. When my legs are already tired and complaining at mile eighteen and I still have eight to go. When my feet hurt from the pounding. When painful blisters form. When, during the first few hours after the race, my stomach feels queasy. When I do the "marathon shuffle" from the tight, fatigued muscles. When I look for the handicapped stall in the bathroom because of my sore quads. *Why am I doing this? After all, no one else is pushing me.*

It took a lot of thought for me to sort it out for myself, but I concluded that there were several answers.

One of the obvious reasons was my health. My internal age is lower than most women in their late sixties. For example, my resting pulse rate is around fifty and I take no prescription drugs. My doctor says that my skeletal system, cholesterol levels, cardiovascular system, and mental health all benefit. Throw in weight management and a healthier diet, and I have many physical reasons to continue this obsession.

Beyond that, though, other factors come into play. If I didn't attempt anything difficult, I wouldn't find the wonderful satisfaction that comes with accomplishment. The events that challenge us the most are the ones that provide the greatest rewards. I've always taken pride in performing my tasks well, from my several jobs to sewing to gardening. But long-distance running is different. More challenging than anything else I've attempted, it's a singular endeavor in the sense that I alone have to take every step, from the training to the event. For me, that makes the journey all the more gratifying. Others can give support, but no one else can do the miles.

Another significant reason is the social aspect. We runners share a camaraderie that few others understand. How many people outside the running community know what mile twenty-two feels like? I look forward to the next marathon because I'll probably see runners with whom I share common experiences. Whatever my current running problem is, it's likely I'll see someone else who has had something similar and who will give me advice. Even as I continue to learn myself, I happily pass along what I already know to new marathoners. I only hope I can give back as much as I've gained from those who have mentored me.

We runners—especially those of us in the back of the pack— understand there is no absolute scale of performance, but that on any given day we all go out to do the best we can. My 50-State friends are spread throughout the United States, and I don't exaggerate when I say that they, along with many Marathon Maniacs, are my extended family. Runners tend to encourage each other—perhaps more than in most other sports. We celebrate one another's victories and commiserate with one another's difficulties. We inspire each other to achieve more than we thought we ever could.

But having realized those benefits, I was unaware that one more special prize lay ahead—something totally unexpected and delightful.

Meanwhile, I was adding to the marathon count, doing a few more each year than the year before. I planned to do my 100th marathon at the Yakima River Canyon Run in Yakima, Washington, on April 2, 2011. Bob and Lenore Dolphin, the race directors of that event, were also the sponsors of the 100 Marathon Club of North America. What better place to reach that milestone?

It turned out that I overshot. After I planned my schedule so that my 100th would be at Yakima, I had an opportunity to do one more with friends. The week before Yakima, I did the Ocean Drive Marathon in New Jersey for number 100, making Yakima my 101st. Nevertheless, it was joyful to be welcomed into the 100 Marathon Club.

Now that I had completed all the states and reached the 100-marathon goal, I continued my journey toward a second round of the states. Along the way, I set another goal—that of completing 200 marathons. I started to pay more attention to numbers than states, and so I started to schedule events more frequently. In 2009, I completed fifteen marathons, which at one time I would have thought was a lot. In 2010, I did a total of nineteen, more than I had ever done in one year and which seemed impressive at the time.

In 2011, I increased my count to thirty-two, thanks in part to ending the year with seven marathons in seven consecutive days. The week-long event was the Savage Seven, organized by Chuck Savage of Ocala, FL. It started the day after Christmas and ran through New Year's Day.

In 2010, the first year of the event, I attempted to complete all seven days, but developed bad blisters on the first day and only completed three runs. It was joyous redemption to complete all seven days in my second attempt.

And in 2012, I maintained the count with thirty-one, even without the aid of the Savage Seven. I was the race director of the event that year, which meant I couldn't run all of the days.

Doing more runs meant meeting more people, and caused me to gravitate to others who also ran even more frequently and racked up high numbers. Those people tended to show up at the same events. I started to refer to these people as the ones who were "on the circuit."

One of those runners was Jim Simpson.

I can't remember exactly when I met Jim, but I had seen him from time to time over several years. I knew he ran a lot of marathons each year, and spent months at a time on the road, living in his pick-up camper. A quiet man, he was known as one the nicest runners around. He never bragged, but remained humble about his amazing accomplishments. Jim had long been one of the legends in the marathoning community, and became the first American to reach 1000 lifetime marathons on January 1, 2013.

Having run with Jim several marathons, I found him to be quiet and genuine. He always had a positive outlook, and I heard him often complimenting and encouraging other runners. Jim appeared to enjoy his solitary life. I had never sensed that he was interested in a relationship with anyone, let alone me. In January 2013 we ran together for most of the First Light Marathon in Mobile, Alabama, during which we shared how content we were with our lives. I enjoyed my tutoring business, my writing groups, and my running. Jim enjoyed his life on the road and his running. I remember telling him that I was happy with my life most of the time. I recall Jim responding with something similar.

So I was surprised to get this email from Jim, sent on May 3, 2013:

Hi Bettie,

I see that we both will be at the Potomac River Run Marathon this weekend. I am going to take the DC start and you MD start...

I would like to run with you for a while (as long as I can keep up...smile). I plan to finish just under the 6 hour cut-off time, maybe 5:55. I think both DC & MD blend in together a short distance from the start. My plan is to run a little faster at the start to get ahead and then after the blend point, slow down until we meet and then go ahead on the cut off pace of 13:43.

Good luck and have a happy day,

Jim.

As indicated in Jim's message, there were two different starts for that race—one in Maryland for those who needed that state, and another in D.C. for those who wanted to claim the marathon for that district. I planned to take the Maryland start and Jim planned to take the D.C. start. The courses joined after about two miles.

Many marathon web sites maintain a list of the entrants, so it didn't surprise me that he knew I'd be there. My first thought was, *Hmm, Jim must want to talk about some running event, probably Savage Seven.*

We had both participated in an event called Savage Seven which consisted of seven marathons in seven consecutive days. I was one of the board members of this event. He had chatted with me before about what he would like to see in the future. Thinking he must have another idea, I replied:

Hi Jim,

I'd love to share the road with you. I'm worried about meeting the cut-off [time], so maybe you can pull me. I'll look for you at the blend, if I don't see you before. I look forward to seeing you Sunday.

Bettie

Just after I arrived at the start location on race morning, our mutual friend Frank arrived and promptly told me, "Hey, Bettie. I ran with Jim yesterday and he said to tell you he wants to run with you today." I wondered if maybe Jim had not gotten my response.

Then a couple we knew arrived and came over right away to say, "Oh, Bettie, we ran with Jim yesterday. He said to be sure to tell you that he wants to run with you today. He'll go out fast and then wait for you at the merge."

Whatever he wants to talk about must be important. I wonder what it is.

Not long after the courses merged, I spotted Jim a little way ahead. He was walking. I quickly caught up to him and he agreed to my walk/run routine of alternating running and walking every thirty seconds. I knew Jim was quiet and that it might take him some time to get around to the reason he wanted to run with me. I was prepared to be patient, but after more than four miles had gone by, we had only exchanged trivial chit-chat. He hadn't brought up any topic in particular.

Then he reached for my hand when we were walking, grinned and said, "I need you to warm my hand." It was very cold, so I didn't mind warming it. I nearly bumped into him at one point, and when I apologized he smiled as he said, "But I kind of liked it." Then he changed sides so I could warm his other hand. *Is he flirting with me? This is the last thing I expected!*

Oh, my. I was confused. I had liked Jim a lot for at least a couple of years, and looking back I realized I would have liked to be more than friends. But I never allowed my thoughts to go in that direction because I was so convinced that he wasn't interested in anything more than a casual friendship. I didn't want to risk making him uncomfortable by showing more interest than he wanted. And, truthfully, I didn't want to be disappointed if he rejected my attention. It was true that he had given me a quick kiss on the lips occasionally, but I didn't take it as a romantic gesture, but rather as affection for a friend. I assumed he did the same with other good friends.

But now, I wasn't sure what was happening.

We were again holding hands as we approached an aid station, and I heard one of the volunteers tell another one, "Oh, look how cute. They're holding hands." *Will he withdraw his hand or not? I think I'll have my answer now.*

Jim did *not* withdraw his hand. Instead, he squeezed my hand tighter and smiled at me. My heart fluttered as I realized he was definitely flirting. I suddenly felt like a fifteen-year-old school girl. Nervous. Excited. Tongue-tied. *Oh, my.*

We held hands off and on for the rest of the run. A little while after I grasped his intent, I tried to sound normal as I asked, "What kind of books do you like?" *What a lame question.*

But a comfortable calm soon settled between us. We focused on our pace and I realized I felt surprisingly content with him. I stopped trying to force conversation and enjoyed the silent communion.

We finished in 5:37, a fast time for me and securely under the six hours he needed. After we crossed the finish line hand-in-hand and were eating post-race snacks, Jim asked if he could run with me again next week at the Delaware Marathon. *He not only knew I'd be here today, but he also checked my schedule for next week. Hmmm.* Of course, I said yes, I'd very much like to run with him again.

I was shocked at how often I thought of Jim during the following week. I was very content with my life. On those few occasions that I'd thought it would be nice to have someone to travel with, or to have dinner with, I'd quickly batted those thoughts away. I had not been looking for anyone and had, in fact, become quite convinced that I would be alone the rest of my life. What kind of man would put up with my lifestyle? When I'm in town, I'm consumed with my tutoring business. And I'm out of town many weekends, traveling to marathons. Why yearn for something I couldn't have? But I had never considered a relationship with another marathoner with a schedule just as crazy.

Suddenly a whole world of possibility had opened up, along with many questions. Just what does Jim have in mind? Just someone to see occasionally? Someone to travel with once in a while? Someone to run with? Something more than that?

I could hardly wait to see him again.

CHAPTER THIRTY-TWO

For the Delaware Marathon, I flew into Philadelphia and met Cyd, a friend from California. We shared a car and a room in Wilmington, and I told her about my "date" to run with Jim. Since her flight was much earlier than mine, I was a little concerned about my finish time. I needed to finish in under six hours in order for Cyd to get to the airport on time.

I met Jim at the start and we mostly walked the first few miles. But when I realized how slow we were, I said, "I'm enjoying this easy pace and being with you, but I might have to speed up the second half so that I can finish in time for Cyd's flight."

"I understand. Just do what you need to do."

I wanted to stay with Jim for the rest of the course, though. His quiet, easy-going manner made me so comfortable, and the talk flowed easily. The hand-holding continued, and he soon progressed to putting his arm around my shoulder every so often. It felt natural to put my arm around him. Because he's six-one, and I'm five-three, my arm comfortably reached his waist. I liked his company a lot and I didn't want to leave him.

"Too bad I didn't tell Cyd to leave my things at the finish area. Then I could have taken my time today. With so many 50-Staters here, I'm sure I could find a ride to the airport." That run had been designated as a 50 States reunion run, which meant there were many friends there, any number of whom would have been happy to give me a lift.

Jim put his arm around my shoulder and squeezed. "I know someone who would not only take you to the airport, but who would take you to the Y for a shower and then to get something to eat."

"Really? And who might that be?" I smiled up at him.

"I'd like to have more time with you."

"I wish there was a way to get a message to Cyd."

As luck would have it, no more than ten minutes later Cyd and I met on an out-and-back part of the course. I rushed to her. "Please leave my luggage at the finish. Jim will take me to the airport."

"Aren't you worried about security?"

"No. It'll be all right. Just put my things in one of the tents and I'll find them."

She smiled at the two of us and said she'd be happy to do that. I was then able to stay with Jim at our leisurely pace.

After we finished, he helped me find my luggage and we walked to his truck with the camper on the back. He drove us to the YMCA and, as we were walking in, he said, "Now I'm slow, so take your time. Don't hurry because of me."

"Yes, but you probably don't take much time with your hair or makeup."

He patted the cap he always wore. "I don't have any hair."

"That's okay." I smiled at him. "It doesn't make any difference to me."

He squeezed my hand and we paused for a moment. "You know we've reached the age when we've lost our youthful looks. But I wasn't looking for that. I was looking for someone with a good heart. You have a good heart."

I don't even remember what I said in response to that, but I remember thinking, *You've just shown me that it's you who has a good heart.*

From the Y, we went to lunch and as we sat across from each other, I looked at him through a different lens. His blue-gray eyes were so innocent and sincere, his smile so sweet and genuine, that my heart started to melt. I don't remember everything we talked about, but I do remember he made me feel at ease. We discovered that we had quite a few things in common. My respect and admiration for Jim grew, as did my sense of connection with him.

After lunch, we had time for a leisurely drive to the airport, during which he held my hand most of the time. I found that the quiet between us was just as comfortable as talking. I was glad for the silences, because my mind was still giddy from his attention. *I must have earned an awful lot of good karma for someone as nice as Jim to want me.*

When we stopped at the airport, Jim held my hand and looked at me. He hesitated a moment before he said, "I want you to know something.

I'm not the kind of guy who will settle down and stay in one place. I intend to keep on traveling most of the year, driving from marathon to marathon."

"I understand. I wouldn't expect you to change your lifestyle."

"I don't want you to be disappointed. But I think if we plan it right, we'll be able to get together fairly often. I'll send you my schedule for the rest of the year, and we'll see what we can come up with."

I could tell he had given this a lot of thought. *For how long? Did this start at the January marathon in Mobile?*

"I understand, Jim. I know you have big goals, and I know you enjoy your lifestyle. I certainly don't expect you to change. I enjoy running with you, though, and I hope we'll be able to arrange more marathons together. I'd like that."

Jim squeezed my hand, smiled, and then leaned over for a kiss. My heart melted a little more.

Standing outside, we hugged tight and kissed a couple of times. Reluctant to pull away, I said, "I might email you a few times, if you don't mind."

"I don't mind at all." He smiled.

The next day, I thought it only polite to email a thank-you to Jim. I sent this:

Hi Jim,

I hope your quads are getting better today, although I know if it was me, tomorrow will be the worst day.

Thanks again for taking me to the Y for a shower, and then to lunch, and then to the airport. Most of all, thank you for your company. You're very easy to be with.

I'm extremely flattered that you wanted to run with me that last two weeks.

I wish you good weather and easy travel for this weekend. I'll be thinking of you. In fact, I like to think about you. It makes me smile. One more thing before I have to get back to work--I sure did like your kisses and hugs.

I look forward to the next time we're in the same place. I hope you'll tolerate my company again.

Bettie

He responded right away, with this.

Hi Bettie,

Thank you for your concern. I feel a lot better today. Capon has a lot more hills (mountains...smile) than our normal street marathons. I will be fine for my 8 in 9 days starting this Thursday.

The pleasure is all mine. Running with you and lunch, too, made a happy day for me...smile.

I look forward to running many more marathons with you and with even more hugs and kisses...smile.

I will be thinking of you and will look forward to seeing you the next time too, and just so you know, you are a great hugger and kisser...smile.

Jim

That started a steady flow of emails, which included planning for our next meeting. Jim had an ambitious goal for his marathon count in 2013, so he had little wiggle room in his tightly packed schedule. My schedule, on the other hand, was fairly flexible. Soon Jim sent me his marathon schedule for the rest of the year. After some discussion, we decided the next opportunity to be together would be in Missoula, Montana, on July 14—eight weeks from the time we started planning the trip.

Meanwhile, we were learning a lot about each other through the many emails that were flying back and forth. Waiting for Missoula made me feel like I had as a five-year-old, waiting for Christmas Day and thinking it would never arrive. But it finally did, and, oh, how it was worth the wait! Our weekend together was magical, much more than I could have imagined. Jim is normally thrifty—like me. But for this trip, he traded in his usual budget motel in favor of an upscale hotel. He said, "I wanted this weekend to be special."

Special it was. Jim was thoughtful, tender, and very affectionate. My heart melted completely as I acknowledged the deep feelings I had for him. I knew I had liked and respected him all along, but I had not allowed myself to feel anything beyond that. Apparently deeper, romantic longings had been hiding under the surface, and now were allowed to spring free. I can honestly say that I'd never had a more romantic weekend in my life.

When Monday morning came and it was time to go home, I had mixed feelings. I didn't want to leave him. Everything I had learned about him in those two days made him even more appealing. I wanted more time with him.

On the other hand, Jim had made me so happy I felt as if I could float home without the aid of the plane. In the airport, we sat at my gate kissing and hugging without regard for what anyone might think. We only had eyes for each other. Even though it was hard to walk away from him, I took with me a heart bursting with joy.

Our next time together was seven weeks later on Labor Day weekend near Jim's home in Huntington Beach, California. Near the end of that wait, I decided that seven weeks or longer was just too long apart. I wanted to see him more often than that. My priorities were shifting. If seeing him more often meant more time out of the office, it would be worth it.

The weekend in California was even more wonderful than Missoula had been. First, we had more time together—four whole days. Second, we ran together three days, which was more fun than I could possibly have anticipated. During the first run (actually more walking than running), I told Jim about taking my family zip lining and tubing. Jim said, "I'd love to do that with you. That's one of the things I've always wanted to do, but didn't have anybody to do it with."

"Great. I think it would be loads of fun to go zip lining with you. I think you'd like it."

"How do you feel about bungee jumping?"

"I'd like to try bungee jumping."

Jim stopped abruptly, grabbed my arm, and pulled me to him. "Oh—Oh—Oh—you just get better and better. I didn't know you were so adventurous." He gave me a big smooch and then hugged me tight.

He then stood back. "I hope you don't mind that I kissed you right here. I know some people don't like public displays of affection, but they're just going to have to get used to it. If I want to give my sweetheart a hug and kiss, I'm going to do it."

I didn't mind at all. I didn't care what anyone might say or think, either. As it turned out, we got many positive comments and no negative ones. We have kept up this habit and continue to get many remarks, such as, "Aren't they cute?" "You guys are adorable." "Aw, how sweet!" "Oh, they're holding hands." Jim says that we're a good example of how older people can still feel like teenagers when it comes to being in love.

The next big experience for me was staying with Jim in the camper. We planned to do the New Hampshire Marathon on Saturday in Bristol and the Maine Marathon on Sunday in Portland. Jim seemed a little nervous that I might find the camper too small or lacking in creature comforts. I told him, "Don't worry so much. I'm not that delicate."

Jim picked me up at the Manchester, NH, airport on Friday and we drive to Bristol for the Saturday race. The start and finish of the race is at the middle school, which has a large parking lot. While Jim situated the truck, he grinned as he said, "I've done this race so many times that I think of this corner as my spot. I'm glad to see no one has taken it."

Until then, I still had not been inside the camper. After we were parked, we got out of the truck and headed back to the camper. When we were both standing near the door, Jim asked, "Can I have a minute before you come in?"

"Sure."

A couple of minutes later, he opened the door and said, "Okay, you can come in now. Let me help you."

I took his hand and climbed up into the camper. The first thing I saw was flowers on the table. He grinned as he said, "I wanted to welcome you to my home." Under the flowers lay a beautifully framed photo of us that a friend of his had taken in California.

"Aww, Jim. You are so sweet."

"Hey, nothing's too good for my sweetheart." He pulled me to him and hugged me close.

"Now let me show you the important things to know about the camper." He showed me where the light switches were, how to turn on the pump for water pressure, and a few other features of the camper. Then he explained that he had looked for a sturdy step for me to get up to the bed, which extended over the cab of the truck. His long legs had no problem stepping up that far, but he was concerned that my shorts legs couldn't make it in one step. He had bought a small trash can that made the perfect step for me. He had also bought new sheets and made a few other arrangements for my comfort.

My heart went pitter-patter at how carefully he had planned for me and at how thoughtful and romantic he was.

In spite of his concerns, I enjoyed sharing the camper with him. I'm still learning the ways of RV life, but so far I have found the camper to be cozy and yet convenient. It's handy to have all the necessities with you. I can understand why he considers the camper more his home than his actual house.

As of this writing, in early 2014, we've shared the road many times and enjoyed more stays in the camper. A couple of times, when we didn't have a run the next day, he surprised me by getting a room. He grinned and said, "I like to get my money's worth. When we have more time, I like for you to have more comfort."

We've had great fun discovering the many things we have in common. Jim describes himself as "a simple person." I think of myself like that, too. We have both wanted to try new, exciting adventures, but neither of us has had a playmate to do enjoy them with. We're both thrifty—or at least careful to get our money's worth. We're both picky about a few things, but nothing that bothers the other one. And we've fallen deeply in love.

When I realized Jim used the word "sweetheart" in a particular way, he explained, "Anybody can have a girlfriend. But not everyone has a sweetheart. I tell people that you're my sweetheart because that means I have you in my heart." I couldn't say it any better.

During one of our early weekends together, Jim made an offhand remark. "I need to get you wearing red shirts." Jim has long been known for wearing red shirts and black shorts or tights—his characteristic colors. My only trademark color was my pink cap.

I was so flattered that he wanted us to dress alike that the decision was easy for me. The tradition of the pink cap began when I was with Paul. Even though I still cherished memories of him, he had been gone for nineteen years. It was time to let go of a symbol of that relationship and adopt the trappings of this new relationship with Jim. I freely traded in my pink cap for a white one and bought a supply of red shirts and black running skirts.

The next time I ran without Jim, I thought about what to wear. Even though we weren't together, I still wanted to wear his colors. I told Jim, "I feel like a high school girl wearing her boyfriend's class ring. I want to tell the world that I belong to you."

We've begun to think about our travel for next year and beyond, and intend to include some fun trips along with many more marathons. In time, we want to go bungee jumping, zip lining, and hot air ballooning. We want to race go-carts and ride Ferris wheels. We plan to hike both the Grand Canyon and Half Dome in Yosemite National Park. We want to spend more time in Alaska and hike the Appalachian Trail. We want to go to Machu Pichu. Our plans are endless.

Even though we each modified our running schedules in order to be together, Jim still managed to do a remarkable 205 marathons in 2013. He was second behind Larry Macon for the most marathons run in a calendar year. And I reached my 200th lifetime marathon at the First Light Marathon in Mobile, Alabama, on January 12, 2014.

My newest, long-range target is to be listed in the USA Mega Marathon Ranking List, a list of those who have done 300 or more marathons or ultras. At the end of 2013, there were only twenty women on that list. I want to see my name in that group. For that, I'll obviously need to complete at least 300 marathons.

To get me to that total, I plan to do at least seventy marathons in 2014. In order to add to my numbers, Jim and I are planning several five-day and seven-day marathon series, in addition to as many doubles as possible. If I can keep going, I hope to reach 300 sometime in 2015.

I no longer wonder why I do this. The reasons are obvious: personal achievement, social connections, travel experience, and now, the greatest reason of all—love. Jim and I both intend to keep running as long as we're able. We have joked that we might one day be out there in our walkers, or racing around the dining room table in our wheel chairs, but neither of us intends to stop any time soon. We're currently having fun working on our new goal—to hug and kiss on a marathon course in every state! We have nearly half the states so far.

Running is a big part of my identity and it continues to add immense joy to my life!

"Life should not be a journey to the grave with the intention
of arriving safely in a pretty and well-preserved body,
but rather to skid in broadside in a cloud of smoke,
thoroughly used up, totally worn out, and loudly proclaiming,
'Wow! What a ride!' "

--Hunter S. Thompson

APPENDIX 1 – Typical Galloway Training Schedule

Week 1:	6 miles
Week 2:	7 miles
Week 3:	8 miles
Week 4:	9 miles
Week 5:	10 miles
Week 6:	12 miles
Week 7:	10 miles
Week 8:	14 miles
Week 9:	10 miles
Week 10:	16 miles
Week 11:	10 miles
Week 12:	18 miles
Week 13:	10 miles
Week 14:	20 miles
Week 15:	10 miles
Week 16:	10 miles
Week 17:	23 miles
Week 18:	10 miles
Week 19:	10 miles
Week 20:	26 miles
Week 21:	10 miles
Week 22:	10 miles
Week 23:	Marathon

CPSIA information can be obtained at www.ICGtesting.com
Printed in the USA
LVOW07s1352220715

447060LV00035B/734/P

9 781938 464027